BRUM
AND
BRUMMIES

BRUM
AND
BRUMMIES

Carl Chinn

BREWIN
BOOKS

First published in 2000 by
Brewin Books, Studley, Warwickshire B80 7LG

Second Impression March 2001

British Library Cataloguing in Publication Data
A catalogue record for this book is available from
The British Library

ISBN: 1 85858 181 8

Typeset in Times and made and printed
in Great Britain by Warwick Printing Company Limited,
Theatre Street, Warwick, Warwickshire CV34 4DR.

CONTENTS

*To all those Brummies who had so
little in their own lives but who
passed on so much to us –
their children and grandchildren.
We should never forget them.*

Chapter 1:

Brummies

A Dreamer's Dream: Herbert Austin

Birmingham is founded upon dreams. A manufacturing centre of the first order, a place of practical people, a city marked out by its overwhelming desire to get things done, still it exists solely because its folk have reached out to grasp their hopes and visions. Acting upon imagination, realising possibilities and bringing into being expectations are the characteristics which bond the folk of Brum whoever they are, wherever they are from and whatever may be their class, creed or colour. And like a wire which is finely and expertly drawn, these characteristics run throughout Birmingham's history. Boulton, Watt and Murdock, the Elkingtons, Joseph Gillott, Josiah Mason, Joseph Lucas – all were men who had dreams which they made come true. Amongst these industrial heroes of Birmingham another name stands out – that of Herbert Austin.

A bowler-hatted Herbert Austin is seated on the front row and is holding a cane. The shot was taken outside the North Works which was erected in 1916 to provide space for machine shops and a forge.

Austin's dream was to build cars for the general public and not just for the rich. Raised in Yorkshire by a farming family, as he stressed later, 'strangely enough, even in my very early years it was for things mechanical I had the greatest love'. He developed his passion for making things after going to Australia as a youngster and serving an engineering apprenticeship. Later he became manager for the Wolseley Sheep Sheering Machine Company. Because of the difficulties with sub-contracted work, the Wolseley relocated to England and Birmingham, where Austin was made manager of the business in 1893. A grafter who was plain in his speech and dress, he was a talented engineer and designer whose mind soared to the possibilities of what might be. His practicality was inspired by vision and on the wall of his office at Longbridge was displayed the belief that 'Most everything worthwhile is born of some dreamer's dream'.

Austin's dream grew stronger at the Wolseley and after work he developed horseless carriages at his home – the first of which was a tri-car, having two wheels at the front and one at the back. A key figure in the development of the car industry in Britain, Austin knew he had to own and develop his own factory if he were to realise his dream. He finally took the plunge in 1905 when he bought a disused works deep in the Worcestershire countryside at Longbridge and which cost £7,750. Austin was determined that his cars would 'represent the embodiment of all the best features in automobile construction'. This meant that 'only the highest class of material will be used'. Importantly, Longbridge differed from most car factories in that it brought together the building of the chassis and various car bodies for fitting.

Sir Herbert Austin sitting in an Austin Seven.

Workers at Longbridge turning out parts for the Austin Seven, 1920s. Thanks to Fred Dorrell.

By early 1906, the Austin Endcliffe was in slow production. Hand built, it was a fully fledged car and a big advance over Austin's first tri-car. The business grew steadily and by 1914, Austin employed 2,000 people who made up to 983 models a year. During the First World War, his factory expanded enormously and Longbridge made a vital contribution to Britain's cause – as a result of which Austin was knighted. But it was during the hard post-war years that Austin gained a peerless reputation as a car designer. By 1921, the severe dislocation caused by the loss of war work had caused profound difficulties for the Austin, and for a short time a receiver was appointed to the business. Aware of the need for a cheaper car, he believed that such a vehicle could save not only the company but also open up driving to a new market. That is why he himself viewed 1922 as the critical year for the future of Longbridge. For it was then that Austin introduced the Seven, a car with a four-cylinder engine (of 747cc) and room for two adults and two children.

This Austin Seven helped to democratise car ownership. Austin himself was convinced that there was a market for a small-sized car, but he was given little encouragement by his committee of shareholders and banks. Consequently, he reverted to the practice of experimentation of his time at the Wolseley: he developed the Seven as an individual. His first design concepts were done at his home of Lickey Grange, after which he instructed Stanley Edge to work on the project. Edge was a draughtsman in the car drawing section of the Longbridge drawing office. A Black

Country lad, he played a vital role in the creation of the Austin Seven. After this period of initial development, the design of the new car was moved secretly to Longbridge where construction began and the board was won over in April 1922.

The Seven was shown to the world in July of that year and Austin proclaimed that it was intended as a decent car for a man who now could only afford a motorcycle and side car and yet was ambitious to buy a motor car. This, 'the motor for the million', came out at £225, but in March 1923 it was reduced to the keenly-priced sum of £165. Advertised extensively as 'Cheaper than Taxis, Shopping a Pleasure', the Seven was a great success and *The Autocar* pronounced that it 'has made motoring possible for thousands who could not otherwise have enjoyed its advantages'. So popular was the car that the question was posed: 'What was more important to the middle class? A baby or a baby Austin?'

Sir Herbert himself recognised the key factor in the success of the Seven. During the First World War, the Americans had taken advantage of the fact that European car producers had focused on war work. This allowed the Americans to gain a good advantage in the immediate post-war years, when British car makers had to concentrate on products for which their factories were now best equipped. For example, Longbridge turned out commercial vehicles, agricultural tractors and twenty horse power cars. But as Austin made plain, the Americans overlooked the need for a small car and 'as soon as it was recognised as a practicable proposition, the Austin Seven was hailed with delight by those people who stood in sore need of mechanical transport but could not afford to pay a big price therefore'.

Significantly, the appeal of the Seven was international. From 1927, the Dixi Company of Germany built a left-handed version of the Austin Seven under licence. The next year, this business was taken over by BMW which continued to produce the Dixi until 1931. From 1928, the Seven also appeared under licence in France. This French version was produced by Lucien Rosengart in the Peugeot factory. Nor was the United States of America immune to the allure of the Seven as from 1929 an American version called the Bantam was brought out. Interestingly, in 1933 the Japanese firm Jidosha-Seizo began building a car modelled on the Seven and called a Datsun. A year later, the Japanese business changed its name to Nissan and after the Second World War it sent a team of engineers to Longbridge to learn how to make the Austin A40 under licence.

The production of the Austin Seven peaked in 1935, after which there was a decline until its output was ceased four years later. By the outbreak of the Second World, 291,000 Sevens had been built. It was a car of dreams. A car which became a reality. A car which transformed not only Longbridge but also the fortunes of other car manufacturers. It was a car of the people and it was made in Birmingham.

Our Lingo: Brummagem Dialect

Picture the stage at the 'Globe' Theatre in London in the last years of the reign of Good Queen Bess. It's a packed audience, as it is for all the plays by our Warwickshire lad, William Shakespeare. And today all these folk have been drawn in by the sharp wit, wonderful speech and sharp insights of a brand new play called 'The Merry Wives of Windsor.' It's Scene III of Act Three and Mistress Ford and Mistress Page are preparing a surprise for Sir John Falstaff, who has been flirting seriously with both these women, even though he knows they are married. Determined to show him up, the ladies have devised a cunning plan to trick him at Mrs Page's house when their two husbands are out. As they prepare for Falstaff's arrival, Mrs Page tells her two servants to bring a washing basket into the room and then instructs them: 'Marry, as I told you before, John and Robert, be ready hard by in the brew-house.'

The greatest writer in the English language was using the same word as we Brummies when he described the communal wash-house in a yard of back-to-backs. And the brew 'us is not the only dialect term which we would recognise in William Shakespeare's work. The tragedy 'Troilus and Cressida', written at the end of the 1500s, is set in the Trojan Wars. In Scene 1 of Act Five, Achilles the great Greek hero is talking to a fellow army commander, Patroclus. They are joined by Thersites, 'a deformed and scurrilous' man marked out by his bad temper and biting invective. Foolishly, Patroclus enters into a slanging match with Thersites, who crushes his opponent with the most scathing crescendo of curses: 'Now the rotten diseases of the suff, the guts-griping ruptures, catarrhs, loads o'gravel in the back, lethargies, cold palsies, raw-eyes, dirt-rotten livers, wheezing lungs, bladders full of imposthuime, sciaticas, limekilns i' th' palm, incurable bone ache and the rivelled fee-simple of the tetter, take and take again such preposterous discoveries!'

In that bile-filled sentence, the first insult is based on a word which would have been understood by every Brummagem kid whose address was 'back of'. The suff refers to the foul stinks and diseases which came out of the drain or the sewer. How many kids in the city went outside to play and harked at their mom shouting: 'Stay away from the suff or you'll get the fever!' Shakespeare is not the only noted writer who used terms with which we would be familiar. Some time in the 1300s an unknown man was responsible for the famous Arthurian epic, 'Sir Gawain and the Green Knight'. Although his name is lost, his words and pronunciations mark him out as someone from the old region of West Mercia – south Lancashire, Cheshire, Shropshire, Staffordshire, Warwickshire and Worcestershire. Early in the poem, an awesome fellow enters King Arthur's hall. He is stared at hard, 'for each mon had marvelled at what it might mean'. I remember clearly that neither my great uncles from Sparkbrook nor my great uncles from Aston called my great-grandads 'the old man.' Always it was the old mon.

The great stranger at Arthur's court challenges any man to strike him with his axe 'so long as I shall have leave to launch a return blow Barlay'. Here the word 'barley' means unchecked, and it's not hard to see how it came to be used by West Midlands kids in their play when wanting a break. Can you remember in a game of tig staving off capture by crossing your finger and bawling out 'barley!' or 'arley-barley!' So many of our dialect words are rooted deep in the history of our region. Take the miskins for dustbins. Used widely in early twentieth century Brummagem, miskin is actually derived from the Old English 'mixen,' meaning a midden and so dates back hundreds of years.

Language is a living thing. It creates words, it throws them out and it grabs hold of new ones. None of us can, or should, fight against that trend. But what we should also not do is abandon our old words just for the sake of fashion or modernity. We should

A woman and children staring at the photographer who is taking this shot in Blews Street sometime in the early 1900s and before the First World War. Despite the bad condition of the housing, the women have tried to make things look a bit better by putting up net curtains. It was in streets such as these that the dialect of Brum was kept alive. Thanks to Birmingham Library Services.

Mrs Hawkesford is certain that 'the alternative English we spoke in the twenties and thirties was colourful and often caused amusement. It was all politically incorrect, but who cared? Most of us knew Standard English anyway – but never used it. I smile to myself now when I remember a person saying to me, "Let's go round our whack". They meant, "Let's go round to our house." I suppose it originated when the landlord gave you a key to a two up and two down house and said, "That's yer whack". The word face got a battering from alternative English, too. Remember fizzog, clock, dial, and kissa? Then there was "What have you dropped your jib for me", which meant that you were displeased or surly. I hope when you reach the esses in your dictionary you don't forget to include sarta and safta. "See you th'sarta" meant "See you this afternoon". More upmarket was "See ya this safta", which meant the same thing. Mrs Hawkesford finishes by declaring that 'Shakespeare would have been proud of us Brummies. Can't we make him patron saint of Birmingham?'

use our dialect terms, nurture them and pass them on to our children's children as they were passed on so preciously to us. So when we're hungry why not say we're clammed? And when we greet our brothers and sister let's call them proudly 'Our Kid' and 'Our Wench'.

This photograph is the front cover of Norman Bartlam's Ladywood *(Sutton Publishing: 1999). Following an appeal for information as to who was in the shot, Theresa Ann Williams replied to state that she is the blonde-haired girl in the centre of the circle of children. She thinks that the snap was taken about 1968 when she was six years old. It shows the youngsters in her yard at the back of Icknield Square, which was off Monument Road, and Theresa thinks they are playing 'The farmer's in his den'. She lived with her Mom and Dad, Jean and David, in the house in the middle of the picture. On the right was the Carter family and to the left was the Douglas household. To the very right of Theresa's house, but not in view, were the toilets which had a fence in front of them. This had a small hole in it at the bottom, so 'I used to climb through it to get to the loos, taking a short cut when needed'. The room on the left is the old brew'us where Theresa's Mom and neighbour did the washing and where 'my Mom used to keep the pram'.*

Across the yard lived Mary Ryan and one of her sons, Martin, also recognised the yard. His Dad kept his BSA Bantam in the brewhouse and Martin recalls that at the bottom of the photograph were the miskins. The lady on the right and not fully in view is Betty Holmes and it is her daughter who is in the foreground and is looking up to her Mom. Her sister, Stella, is on the left of the circle with her back to the houses. Martin feels that the big lad in the middle of the ring is Michael Clements and that he is carrying his little brother, Freddie. Holding the hand of the lad with the black gansey is Rosaline Clements and her sister, Sylvia, is holding the other lad's hand. Martin also recollects the Carters, the Douglases, the Buddings, the Fothergills and the Hills – all of whom lived in the yard.

A cracking shot of a yard in Hanley Street, which runs off the bottom of Summer Lane. Taken in May 1965 it shows the miskins, brew'us and lavatories on the left and a group of women canting in the shadow of the factory in the background. Notice the clean washing on the line. Thanks to the Birmingham Evening Mail.

Doing Your Bit: Brummies Prepare for War

When he'd come home from the last lot, he was like everyone else – he'd thought that he'd played his part in the war to end all wars. It was as if all the suffering and deaths in the Great War had cast out the spectre of conflict, at least within Europe. So he'd thought, and for a decade or more it did seem that peace was here to last. But like many an old soldier, over the last couple or three years he'd begun to get uneasy when he read about what was going on in Germany. He realised that many people said that Hitler was just the kind of strong man who was needed to sort things out in a country that had been almost torn apart by massive inflation and political conflicts. Well, he didn't know about that but he did agree with those who said that Germany had been treated too harshly at the Treaty of Versailles and that Hitler was only trying to redress the balance.

Even so, Hitler seemed too much of a warmonger for his liking. Him and his muckers weren't like old Chamberlain and the French bloke, that what's his name – Daladier. These Nazis were always dressed up in uniforms and they always appeared too het up and ready for a bost-up. And he definitely didn't have no time for those monster meetings which Hitler got up. They were pretty frightening with everyone 'sieg heiling' and the like. Oswald Mosley was trying to do the same thing here and he'd been to one of his meetings up the Bull Ring. He daynt like what he saw nor what he heard. There was plenty there who wanted to have a knock at Mosley, only heckling like, but every time someone shouted out they were jumped upon and duffed up by black-shirted fascists. In the finish it had turned into a right dust up with some Communists and others fighting back.

He'd come away sick to his back teeth. He hadn't given up his youth to see people knocked about because they wanted to say summat. After all, that's what him and all the rest had fought for worn it? Free speech. That's why so many lads now lay beneath the fields of Flanders. If you daynt have free speech then what were their deaths for? Mind you, he never dreamed that things would get s'bad that another war was on the cards. Even when Hitler had sent his planes over Spain to help that Franco and then invaded Austria he'd thought that we'd soon stop his gallop. But we never did and he knew why. We wornt ready. It was as simple as that. It was all very well them having a go at Neville Chamberlain and saying he was weak, but no one wanted another war and any road up, the Prime Minister, knew he hadn't got the weapons to fight. He'd had some right barneys in the pub over that one, especially when Chamberlain had agreed to the Germans taking over part of Czechoslovakia and had come back from Munich a year ago waving that piece of paper and saying we had peace in our time. There was plenty who'd reckoned that Chamberlain had given Hitler the go-ahead to do what he wanted. But he stood his ground, especially when he saw the shadow factory that was going up on the Cov just past the Swan and heard that things were happening at the Austin. He knew then that these places were for war work and he felt strongly that Chamberlain had realised what Hitler's game was and was trying to buy us time.

Mind you, the fact that he'd worked out that war was coming didn't make it any easier when the announcement came. Chamberlain had just sorted out an alliance with Poland, cus it was obvious that Hitler had his eyes on that place. But within six days the blighter went and invaded Poland anyway, taking no notice of our treaty. Them Poles gave it all they'd got. My God, they was brave. It nearly made him blart to think how their cavalry had charged against the tanks of the Germans. Them lads knew they'd got no chance but they went ahead and died for their country. There was no way we could let them down. He daynt care that Poland was across the other side of Europe. They'd got guts and we had to back them. If we daynt, then we might as well pack up because we'd given in to the bully and that was one thing his old mon had always taught him. Never let a bully get away with it. Stand up to him and be a man, even if you do take a pasting.

And that's what we had to do now. Stand up for what was right. Two days later, on Sunday September 3, 1939 word had gone round out that the Prime Minister was going to make an announcement at eleven o'clock that morning. Like everyone else in the land, he called the family in and bent over the wireless to fiddle with the knobs to make

Workers sandbagging the Education Offices of Birmingham City Council in Margaret Street on August 6, 1939, four weeks before the declaration of war. This indicates the awareness amongst the authorities that war was inevitable. Amongst the other major buildings protected by sandbags were the Town Hall and the Council House. The trams are coming up Margaret Street from Great Charles Street. Thanks to the Birmingham Evening Mail.

A photograph of air raid practice at the factory of Joseph Lucas in Great King Street. It was taken by Mr W.R. Lloyd. The Lucas factory made a wide variety of goods which were essential for the United Kingdom's war effort. These included electrically operated traversing gear for rotating gun turrets; rotary transformers for feeding wireless sets on aeroplanes; Spitfire wing sub-assemblies; anti-aircraft shells; PIAT anti-tank gun bombs; and sten gun magazines. Lucas was also responsible for pioneering work on the combustion and fuel systems of the gas turbines for the Gloster Meteor, the first production jet aircraft. Unsurprisingly, Lucas was targeted by German bombers and, along with other munitions factories, was hit during a terrible raid on November 19, 1940 when 350 enemy planes hammered Brum.

the reception as good as possible. Satisfied, he filled his pipe and lit it and went and leaned against the mantelpiece. Chamberlain's voice crackled over. He told them that the United Kingdom and France had given Hitler an ultimatum: withdraw German forces from Poland or else suffer the consequences. The ultimatum had been ignored and so 'we are now at war with Germany'. That was it. It had been coming for the past few years. And now it was here. He daynt want it, but one thing was sure – like every other Briton he was ready to do his bit for his country.

Nurses and ARP volunteers at the First Aid Post in Handsworth. Thirty-two such posts were set up across the city in order to supplement the services provided by hospitals. Most were in public baths and schools and the aim was that no-one with minor injuries suffered in an air raid should be more than a mile from a first aid post where there were qualified nurses, auxiliaries and members of the Women's Royal Voluntary Services for Civil Defence. These posts were vital in providing medical help to the thousands of Brummies who were injured during the Blitz. Thanks to the Birmingham Evening Mail.

Having to Leave Home: Evacuees

He held her donny tightly, just as he'd been bidden to. With his other hand he grasped a small, worn suitcase packed with a couple changes of clothes for the pair of them. As he strode along hoping to be like a man, he looked down at the young girl almost hopping and skipping to keep up with him: 'Alright, bab. We're nearly there now and see! Our Mom and Dad are there before us!'

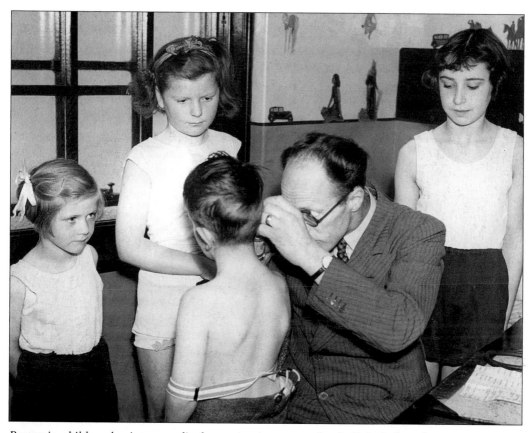

Brummie children having a medical examination at a school clinic before they are evacuated. Thanks to the Birmingham Evening Mail.

Along with thousands of other children, Norman Bailey and his sister were evacuated from Pitsford Street Goods Station in Hockley. They went with Camden Street School, Brookfields, 'not knowing where we would end up, but after an arduous but exciting journey we arrived at Monmouth, South Wales. From there we went by car to a small village called Raglan. My sister and I were separated and I went into a cottage on the Usk Road. The couple that took me in were wonderfully kind. Next day I had another great surprise. Mr Reece Roberts took me to work with him. To my great delight he was the caretaker of Raglan Castle. From hereon I had a castle to play in, imagine how a young boy of eleven years who had never been in the country before felt, free to roam at will... I have never enjoyed my youth as much as then. Unfortunately it only lasted for about three months when the "Phoney War" was on and we were brought back by our parents and had to suffer the horrors of the Blitz.'

Like so many other parents, they'd made their way to the school that Saturday September 2, 1939 to watch their kids assemble in the playground ready to be evacuated. None of them wanted it to happen but all the authorities reckoned it had to be done before the Germans started dropping bombs. There was nothing else for it but to make sure the kids went off safely. Concern creased into their faces and care caught in their eyes, the moms and dads had looked on as the teachers had doled out gas masks and instructions and then they'd made their way to the station to wave their last

Brummie children gathering at Moor Street Station on September 1, 1939 ready for evacuation. Notice their luggage and the fact that each child has a label around his neck. This gave their name and school. The first evacuation train left Brum at 8.20 a.m. that morning and although all journeys began from New Street, Snow Hill or Moor Street, stops were made at local stations. Tearful mothers were not allowed on to the platforms. Thanks to the Birmingham Evening Mail.

John Williamson lived with his grandmother and 'when evacuation was mentioned I was first on the list, being taken to, I believe, Aston Station and along with lots of other kids put on a train. Many tears were shed by all of us, including my grandmother. Destination unknown. I was sent to Crewe. I remember a large house, some lord's place I believe, with large gardens and a big pool full of fish and a rowing boat that they took us out on… We slept in large rooms turned into dormitories. At night you could hear the kids crying. It was a sad time for all of us but I believe we made the most of it.'

Carrying their luggage in their pillow cases, two little Brummie evacuees set off along the platform at the railway station ready to be evacuated in November 1940. Thanks to the Birmingham <u>Evening Mail</u>. Following the first evacuation of September 1939, many children returned home during the 'Phoney War' period when there was little activity in the war. Indeed, by January 1940 at least 93% of elementary schoolchildren were back in Brum. As a consequence, most Brummie children were at home during the Blitz which hammered Brum from August 1940. In November of that year, the east side of the city was bombed so badly that it was rendered almost waterless and with the risk of epidemics growing, 22,000 children were evacuated between 26 November and 10 December.

Like a lot of kids, Alf Morton and his brother soon returned home after their evacuation to Malvern from Elkington Street School, Aston. Living in a neighbourhood which was bombed heavily, he was evacuated again in 1940 – this time from Summer Lane School and with his sister, Doreen. They were taken to Wolverley, near Kidderminster, 'a very small village at the time'. The Christmas of 1941 saw Alf in Kidderminster Hospital and 'I can well remember it snowing very heavy at the time. My foster father… monitored the pressure of Birmingham's water supply. He was in the Home Guard.'

goodbyes. As they waited outside the entrance, the little wench fastened her eyes on her mom – and when she was pushed forward she held a forlorn palm out in the hope that she'd be pulled from the line and took back home. Her mom wanted to badly, but they'd all been warned not to get the kids upset as evacuation was for the best.

Tears welled up in the little uns eyes and she started to grizzle. Her big brother put his arm around her sadly-hunched small shoulders. Almost pleadingly he said, 'Don't blart, bab. Its gonna be alright. Were gonna stick togetha no matter what and I promise I wunt leave y'not once. Aright? And I bet we'll ave a smashing time when were there and Our Mom's bound t'come and see us.' Before he could go on they were shooed onto the train so fast that they only just about had time to turn around and wave weakly to their mom and dad behind the barriers. Then it was off to wherever they were going.

Some of the kids were dead excited, chasing up and down the corridors until they copped out from the teachers. Others were tearful and refused to be cheered up and the rest were like them – staring deeply out of the windows and on to Brum as if they were determined to grab every sight and store it securely in their minds, ready to draw on it as soon as they needed it in the days to come.

It seemed like ages before they arrived at what they were informed was Leicester. Then it was off the train, down the platform and queuing up once more – this time to get into coaches. Bewildered and befuddled, they were chivvied along by teachers who tried their best to gladden the kids who were unhappy. At last they got to where they were going – a little mining village surrounded by fields – but still the jaunt hadn't finished because they had to go to the village hall and line up yet again. Then strange people came in, some of them talking posh, others in a hard to understand accent. These folk went up and down the ranks of Brummie kids, sometimes stopping to tap a child on the head or to nod instructively towards the teacher – and then their pal was gone. It was as sudden and as simple as that.

A couple of times a woman had stopped by them and one had actually said, 'I'll take her'. But as she went to pull the girl away, the lad pulled his sister back and glaring at the woman warned, 'We're sticking togetha! Like our mom said!' Soon they were the only youngsters left and at last the local vicar came up and took them to what they thought was a grand house. He was a kindly man and so was his wife and each day their favourite teacher came to check they were alright. She was lovely and was always ready to give the young girl a cuddle. Yet though they were well looked after they were really homesick.

There were some kids who did settle in fine, but most just wanted to get back to Brum. And they did get back. By January 1940 at least 93 per cent of primary school children had returned from evacuation. Within months they would be caught up in the air raids which made Birmingham the second-most heavily bombed city in the United Kingdom. We should never forget.

'Slasher Green': The Great Sid Field

Just eight years old, Sid Field had them packing into the back garden of his mom and dad's house in Osborne Road, Sparkhill. It seemed as if all the local kids were there, paying to get in with a cigarette card so as to see their pal take off Charlie Chaplin and other comics. Sid was a right case and had them in fits of laughter. Mind you, sometimes his capers got him into hot water – like when he performed outside the local paper shop. He drew such a crowd that the local bobby decided to tick him off for causing an obstruction. Worriedly, Sid scarpered down the road in his dad's old trousers and boots 'with the old copper after me like a carthorse'.

Soon after that, Sid began his search for stardom. Still a kid, he entertained the mothers' meeting at the local church hall, and then aged eleven he got a job in Oldham with the 'Fourteen Royal Kino Juveniles'. He set off with his belongings in a Japanese rush basket, but a few days later he was back home in tears. Stage fright and home sickness had overcome him. But Sid's mom was determined that her son's bashfulness would not stifle his natural ability. She made him return to the 'Juveniles' and in June 1916 he made his first theatrical appearance at the 'Bristol Empire'.

In the succeeding years, Sid toured and also appeared at social concerts at Moseley Road Baths, where his mom stood in the wings in case he panicked. He needed her resolve, for even in a small part at the 'Bordesley Palace' he'd sometimes blart before he went on stage. For all his anxieties, everyone who met him knew that Sid Field had a rare talent and in 1920, aged sixteen, he became the lead juvenile in a circus. It wasn't

Sid Field as his character 'Slasher Green' saying 'T'aint arf a nice bit o' clot'. This shot was taken in Sid's dressing room in the 'Theatre Royal' in Birmingham. Thanks to the Birmingham Evening Mail. Rita Bill's uncle, Leslie Amiss, used to recount wonderful tales about old Small Heath where he was born, and also used to talk about the times when he knocked about with Sid Field.

At one time, both of them were bouncers at the snooker hall which was on the corner of Stratford Road and Showell Green Lane, Sparkhill – earning 'the enormous sum of a half a crown a night'. Leslie said that Sid was a lovely man and he used to visit the comedian after he became famous.

a success and Sid was stranded at Wrexham. Luckily some of the circus horses were from Henley-in-Arden and so he cadged a ride back to Warwickshire and then traipsed the rest of the way home.

Gradually Sid gained confidence and aged eighteen he knocked on the stage door of the 'Theatre Royal' in New Street and asked the manager, Philip Rodway, for a job in 'Puss in Boots', that winter's panto. Sid had only four speaking lines and a silent scene with the principal 'boy'. As she sang 'Shufflin' Along', Sid shuffled behind her. With his face blacked and a top hat on his head, he turned a serious spot into a hilarious sketch.

Yet success did not rush to grab Sid. For years he had to collar for everything he got and only slowly did his reputation rise. Then, in 1938, something happened which was to help launch him into stardom. Sid went down the Blues and stood by a bloke wearing a long black coat, wide-brimmed hat and yellow shoes. He looked a proper spiv. Sid watched the chap intently, taking in his mannerisms, style of speech and actions. Without knowing it, the spiv gave Sid the idea for 'Slasher Green', one of the greatest comic creations of British music hall. Like all Sid's characters, 'Slasher' was

Mrs M.A. Peacock found this smashing snap amongst family snaps belonging to her late mother. Sid Field is second from the left in the photo which was taken after the wedding of Bill Patrick, for whom Sid was best man. Bill and Sid were great pals and the Patricks were well known as bookies in Stour Street, Spring Hill. The family also ran a grocery shop in Stewart Street. Bill Patrick is fifth from the left and his wife Lily is fourth from the left. Third from the right is Elsie Patrick and next to her is Price Patrick junior.

Evelyn Hubball, née Power, well remembers Sid Field coming to the 'Odeon', New Street whilst his film 'London Town' was showing. Excitedly, she pinned her hair into plaits across her head 'like one of the chorus girls in the film – oh those were the days'. The ladies in the photo sent in by Evelyn are Iris Jones, Kitty Jones, Olive Carpenter, Pearl Jones and Ginger Bailey. In their day, the 'Odeon', 'was the showcase of England. It was a beautiful theatre, with its fish tanks, caged birds, its wonderful staircase, and the magnificent chandelier. What splendour!!' Evelyn herself was firstly an usherette and then box office cashier.

a feller who put up a big front to cover up failure. Bouncing along, apparently confident and cocky, he always tripped up over his overcoat.

After years of seeking recognition as a serious comic comedian, Sid finally became an 'overnight success' in 1943 when he appeared in 'Strike A New Note' at London's 'Prince of Wales Theatre'. The audience was won over by his originality, charm, outstanding mimicry, pathos and genuine appeal as a funnyman. Sid had made it and over the next few years he became great friends with Danny Kaye and other major names. But restless for new challenges, he strove for notice as a straight actor. He attained his goal in the play 'Harvey'. So powerful were his performances that Sir Laurence Olivier exclaimed that Sid would have been 'a glorious Shakespearean comic'.

For all this success, Sid never forgot that he was a Brummie, born in Bellbarn Road and brought up in Sparkhill. With his mate Tom Cope of the 'Malt Shovel', he'd pop into Small Heath Social Club where he'd learned to be a good snooker player, and he always kept in touch with Bill Stephens of the 'Greet Inn' and other friends.

Sid Field died on February 3, 1950. He'd gained renown, but one ambition was unfulfilled. Sid had played in all of Brum's theatres bar the Rep. It had been his dream to act in that great venue for serious actors. Fifty years after his death, perhaps the Birmingham Repertory Theatre might welcome the millennium with a play about one of the world's comic geniuses – Sid Field of Brummagem.

The Citizen's Army: The Home Guard

Get rid of those images of a Dad's Army made up of bumblers and fools led by inept and inefficient officers. The Home Guard was nothing like that. It was a well trained citizen's army which helped to defend the nation at the time of our greatest need. Just think back to the dire events of the summer of 1940 when it seemed that the Germans would soon invade. France had fallen and across Europe tyranny was triumphant. From Poland in the east to the Pyrenees in the west and from the Arctic Circle in the north to the Mediterranean in the south, the Nazi aggressors had stamped out freedom. This bleak position was worsened by the neutrality of the United States of America and the non-aggression pact between the USSR and Hitler. The United Kingdom stood alone, steadfastly holding aloft the flickering light of liberty and drawing to it those who strove against the darkness.

Now hark back to the words of Sir Winston Churchill in the midst of those hard days. On July 14, 1940, he broadcast to the world that behind the soldiers of the Regular Army were one million or more Local Defence Volunteers, 'or, as they are much better called, the Home Guard'. A large proportion of them had been through the

Len Drew, who sent in this photo, was in the Home Guard unit at the Norton in Bracebridge Street where W. Hanson, the firm's cashier, was the officer in charge. Len and his pals did two-on, four-off duties once or twice a week and were stationed on the flat-top roof of the factory which had a steel, bell-shaped sentry box to shelter in if the weather was bad. Funnily enough, when Len was called up in October 1942, he was sent to Norton Barracks, Worcester. In this photo, Lieutenant Hanson is in the middle of the front row and Len is sitting on his left.

last war, and all 'have the strongest desire to attack and come to close quarters with the enemy wherever he may appear. Should the invader come to Britain, there will be no placid lying down of the people in submission before him... We shall defend every village, every town and every city.' The men of the Home Guard would have played a vital role. For as Churchill declared, they were ready 'as a means of destruction for parachutists, airborne invaders, and any traitors that may be found in our midst'.

The call for Local Defence Volunteers had been made first in a government broadcast on May 14, the day on which Rotterdam was blitzed and the French defences were breached. Within a week or so, 30,000 Brummies had come forward to do their

Members of the Birmingham City Transport Home Guard 31st and 32nd Warwickshire Birmingham Battalions, providing the guard of honour for the visit of Sir Bernard Montgomery to Birmingham on 9 March 1944. In the line of the soldiers on the right, the man second from the front is the father of Mr R.G. Edkins, whilst the officer to the rear and to the left of the Lord Mayor is Edward Poolten. He worked at as an inspector on Birmingham City Transport and was based at Roseberry Road Depot. On one occasion, Edward was on duty in Frederick Street in Hockley when he spotted a tram going down Newhall Hill to Summer Row. The vehicle had no driver and Edward ran after it, caught it, jumped on and stopped it just before a nasty bend. This information was supplied by William Sedgley who is married to Edward's niece.

Margaret Lee's Dad, Frank Wright, joined up under age in the First World War and stayed in the Royal Artillery until 1927. In the Second World War he was in the Home Guard and was awarded the British Empire Medal for Meritorious Service (Military Division). The Guard Commander (24 G.P.O.) Battalion Home Guard Warwicks, Frank gained his medal for the courage, resource and leadership he displayed during the air raid on Brum on August 26/27, 1940. His efforts materially contributed to the saving of Telephone House and Post Office property.

bit. Given the dreadful occurrences on the Continent where the British forces were retreating to Dunkirk, there was little or no equipment for the volunteers. Parading in their civilian clothes, they carried out their arms drill with broom handles because real weapons were so scarce. Slowly but steadily things improved. Given badges relating to their county regiment, the men were also fitted out with denim overalls and then serge battle-dress. By early 1941 they finally had their own rifles and were organised on army lines with non-commissioned and commissioned officers.

Within Birmingham, the Home Guard was split into groups, each of which was attached to one of the city's 35 police stations. In addition, many managements formed their own 'internal defence units' from their workers to protect their factories. On September 20, 1940 the Birmingham *Mail* reported on one of these forces at an important centre of production. Working in relays, fifteen Home Guard men kept a nightly watch from a look out tower. This 'armoured crow's nest' gave 'an uninterrupted

Between 1939 and 1945, Dennis Blisett was a member of the Warwickshire Cadet Battery Royal Artillery which was based at Stoney Lane Barracks in Sparkbrook. The cadets received basic army training before their call up and street fighting manoeuvres were held with the Home Guard. On a Sunday, the lads would march to the Dingles in Hall Green for field manoeuvres which involved attacking and defending the bridges which crossed the River Cole. Talks were also given by American officers who were stationed in Moseley before D Day. The lads themselves had a cadet house at 124, Wilton Road, Sparkhill, which was also a base for fire watching, and this photo shows some of them playing cards. Thanks to Dennis Blisett.

view of the surrounding country'. Below it was 'a heavy brick-built shelter, provided with look-out or firing embrasures, and in telephonic communications with the works'.

Brum's industries were crucial to the war effort and the government recognised the importance of the Home Guards in ensuring that munitions work was unhindered. At the SU Carburettor plant, the local unit was even given machine guns and an armoured car to carry out its duties. Why? Because carburettors supply engines with petrol and up to the Battle of Britain, all the aero-carburettors for our Spitfires and Hurricanes were made by SU. If the factory had been destroyed then 'the RAF would have suffered a mortal blow'.

Outstanding bravery was shown by many Home Guard men in carrying out their duties – men such as Commander George Inwood. On October 15, 1940 he went twice into the ruins of a bombed house in Bishop Street. Each time he pulled to safety someone who had been trapped in cellar. Heedless of his own safety, he went into danger for a third effort. He collapsed and died of gas poisoning. Posthumously he was awarded the George Cross.

George Inwood and his fellows in the Home Guard were part of no Dad's Army. They were courageous and honourable men who were prepared to give their all for the nation they loved. We should never forget that.

The People's Champion: Wallace Lawler

Like all crusaders, Wallace Lawler was strong in resolve, firm of purpose and impassioned. Determinedly and fervently he set himself to battle against deprivation and injustice. With his feet planted firmly on the blue bricks of the courtyards of Brum, Wallace Lawler had a vision. He dreamed of a country in which young married couples could find a home of their own. He dreamed of a land in which old people would not freeze in the winter because they could not afford to turn on their fires. He dreamed of a nation in which small businesses thrived. Above all, he dreamed of a society from which poverty, bad housing and shattered hopes had been banished.

Born in Worcester in 1912, Wallace Lawler thrust himself into public work when he was just fourteen. Driven forward to graft for the good of others, he founded a large Boys Club Movement in the middle of the city's slums. A year later, he pressurised the local council into loaning the club the corporation's public service vehicles so that 300

Mrs Mary Hooper of Guildford Street, Lozells, was one of the housewives who organised a petition which was presented to the Lord Mayor of Birmingham and which urged that 'barriers are removed to allow Coun. Lawler to serve on the Housing Management Committee, as housing conditions are the most pressing problem in the ward'. (May 1962). Thanks to the Birmingham <u>Evening Mail</u>.

lads could be taken to camp at the seaside. Soon after, and still just sixteen, Wallace Lawler founded England's first Minor Football and Cricket Leagues for pupils of former elementary schools. Amongst the youngsters who enrolled were some who would later become well known sportsmen, including Frankie Moss, Harry Yarnold and Roly Jenkins.

Wallace Lawler left his hometown in 1938. With war looming over Britain, he came to Brum as an aircraft engineer and although he later served in the Worcester Regiment, he made his peace-time home back in our city. He soon made his mark, forming a successful plastics company and rejuvenating Liberalism locally. In the 1800s, Brummies were so staunchly attached to the Liberal Party that it was exclaimed by commentators that 'as the salt is sea so is Birmingham Liberal'. Yet by the late 1940s the influence of the party had declined so much that it did not even have one representative in the Council Chamber. Lawler set about changing this. He became a leading Liberal figure in the West Midlands, holding various important offices. Yet it was not as a party official that he gained his name, it was as the people's defender.

Throughout the 1950s, Wallace Lawler was a defeated candidate in municipal elections – but at last, in 1962 the voters of Newtown Ward showed their trust in a man who had gained their confidence. He was elected as the first Liberal Councillor in Brum for 23 years and immediately he caused controversy. Most of Lawler's constituents lived

Wallace Lawler chatting to some of the kids whose lives he was hoping to change for the better. Taken in June 1969, it shows the people's champion outside his advice headquarters in Farm Street, Hockley. Thanks to the Birmingham Evening Mail.

in Victorian terraced housing, much of which was decaying and unfit. Unsurprisingly, the new councillor was fixed upon becoming a member of the city's housing management committee. The controlling Labour group rejected his wishes and was faced with the anger of the people of Newtown. Led by Louise Collins of Lennox Street, Mary Hooper of Guildford Street and other women, they signed a petition asking the Lord Mayor to ensure that 'the barriers are removed to allow Coun Lawler to serve on the Housing Management Committee'. The memorial of over 1,000 names was rejected and it took another three years of campaigning before Councillor Lawler achieved his objective.

Within months of his election he had eight volunteers helping him to deal with 80 inquiries each night, five nights a week at his housing bureau. Wallace Lawler's commitment to the folk of inner city Brum was matched by their support for him, and in June 1969 they shocked the political world in a by-election when they voted for him to become MP for Ladywood. He was the city's first Liberal MP for 83 years and gained over 50% of the votes cast. It was a triumphant moment and although boundary changes contributed to his defeat in the subsequent general election, Wallace Lawler never lost the faith of those thousands of Brummies who supported him. Sadly, Wallace Lawler died aged just 60 in 1972. Fittingly, his name emblazons the community centre in High Street, Aston.

Wallace Lawler discussing proposed rent increases with Mrs Norris in her general store in Aston. Thanks to the Birmingham <u>Evening Mail</u>.

The Liberal councillor touched the lives of many people, such as Mrs D.J. Smith. Newly-married, with a baby and another on the way in 1956, she and her then husband had nowhere to live and eventually they found themselves on the streets.

With her husband an apprentice engineer and at work, during the day Mrs Smith visited friends, had a meal and washed their clothes. At night-time they slept on New Street Station and used the toilets to change themselves and keep the baby clean: 'Some nights the railway police would come and although they would sympathise with us, still they had their job to do and gently turned us off the station,' she says. 'On those nights we slept in the long arch that used to be on the Hall of Memory. It had a roof covering it and benches and if you sat on the first bench the wall would shelter you from the wind.'

One night the couple went to a meeting for homeless people and met Wallace Lawler, then a Liberal councillor, who chatted to them for quite a while. The next evening, a reporter and a cameraman came to the archway and took their story as well as photos. A day later, their picture was in the Mail. Wallace Lawler found Mrs Smith 'a place with my child in Gem Street Women's Hostel and also found a place for my husband in a man's hostel'. Wallace Lawler did not forget the couple. He later contacted them to state that he had obtained lodgings for them with an old lady called Mrs Josh in Cook Street, Nechells 'where we could stay till I had the baby'.

On the day the baby was due, a letter arrived calling the couple to an interview at the Housing Department in Bush House. The upshot was that they were given a half-way house in Great Brook Street, but only if they could furnish it.

Without the help and support of Wallace Lawler, Mrs Smith doesn't know how things would have turned out.: 'If Councillor Lawler's children see this I just want them to know that I have never forgotten his kindness. Thank God someone took time to listen.'

Our Mom: The Mothers of Brum

It was an image that was imprinted upon their minds and seared into their souls. There she stood, their mom, with her hurden gown covering her frock and the sleeves of her worn blouse rolled up to her elbows. To anyone who knew her, then her fixed eyes gave away the firmness of her resolve. But the means test man didn't know her and nor did he have any inkling as to what was to come when he told her there'd be no money for her until she sold 'that sideboard'. If he thought he'd got a browbeaten, cowed-down woman before him he'd got another thing coming: 'Get rid of that sideboard!', she exclaimed, 'If that's what you think then y'can keep y'r money. My father med me that sideboard when I wed and nothink on earth'll force me to get shut of it. And as for 'ow we'll get on, well I can tell y', while I've got these then my kids'll never goo ungry.'

A Brummie mom in the early years of the 1900s. Thanks to Joyce White.

Teresa Reardon's first memories of her Mom are 'when during an air raid in the last war she would open our door to any of our neighbours who wished to come in. We lived in the bottom corner flat and we felt the safest.' If there was an air raid whilst Teresa was at school her mom 'would fetch me home, saying if any of us were going to go we would all go together. For the same reason she wouldn't let us be evacuated.' Teresa's dad was away for seven years 'so Mom was everything to us. She tried to make sure we didn't miss out on a thing. My Mom was special.'

So too was Pauline Norris's mom. She was Mary Edwards, née Smith, and she came from a fairground background, travelling around the Midlands until she met her chap and settled down in Derby Street, Deritend. She was a very strict woman who would stand no nonsense but she worked hard and lovingly for her kids. Pauline loved it 'when she went to the Rag Market on the tram where she would buy second hand clothes for us. A little alteration here and there and I felt like the "bees knees" at the Saturday dance.' All her life Mary would go up town to buy fish and 'snap a bargain' which she would store in cupboards which her children called Pandora's box. She was a real character and her family loved her.

As she spread out her palms to show her calloused and scraged hands the official took a step back. But there was no way she was going to hit him. What she did want to do was show him that she was mistress of her own fate and that she would never bow her head to no man. She hadn't done it for her husband when he was alive and she was blasted if she was going to do it now to this feller. And use them hands she did, from morning through afternoon and into the night. She took in washing, went out charring, helped out in a coffee house and had homework. Looking back, how ever she managed they could never fathom out. But manage she did and for all her hard collaring she always made sure that there was something on the table. Many's the time she'd put together a filling meal with a few bacon bones, a handful of pot vegetables and a good, thick stock – and many's the time she'd eaten only when the kids had filled themselves.

My Great-Granny Wood with my Uncle Alf as a baby. Granny came from Worcester and with my Grandad Wood settled in Whitehouse Street, Aston, during the First World War. She had twelve children and like so many hard-collaring women, she was a wonderful mother and grandmother. Nothing was too much trouble for her. On a Sunday night she'd do a fry up for all the kids and their pals when they came home from a dance and she was ever-ready with a piece of marge and sugar to give to her grandkids. A tough woman who could hold her own, she laid out the dead in the street, brought the babbies into the world and was a woman wise in old remedies. Imbued with high morals and a zest for life, she inspired her family.

Mrs Walker with her children in the back garden of their home in Bordesley Green. Jane Smith is in her mother's arms. Thanks to Jane Smith.

Sheila Swan's mom, Gladys Williams, née Mantle, was one of ten children who grew up in Dawlish Road, Bournbrook. Her own mom was the woman to whom the neighbours turned in times of trouble, birth or death and anyone in need was welcome.

Gladys herself worked in service from a very early age and met her husband in Cannon Hill Park during the time she was employed as a nanny. Later as a mother herself she cared for her two daughters 'with such love and devotion and despite her limited years of schooling she recognised the importance of education. She deprived herself of material things and saved to buy us books.' Her caring nature stayed with her throughout her life. Now she is gone 'she has left a huge hole in the lives of her family. She never complained about her difficult life and never longed for material goods. The only thing she really cared for was her family and for them she would have fought the world.'

Years after she'd gone, it came back to them how night after night all she'd had was a piece or two dipped in what was left of the gravy. Her selflessness was like so much about her, it only really hit them when they'd got families of their own. Growing up, they'd never thought about how much she'd loved them, but my oath, they knew now that they were moms and dads themselves. Perhaps it was because she'd never told them she'd loved them. Now they could see it all. She'd never had the time to show them affection. Yet through her grafting and scratting she'd showed them all too clearly just how much she'd cared. Half a dozen of them there were and she'd kept them all thanks to the money her brought in from this and that. They were her kids and she fought for them every day of her hard life.

And she fought with high standards. She always made sure that they were scrubbed clean and their clothes were spotless – even if they were rough ganseys and itchy, black stockings from the Police-Aided Fund. Just like she always made sure that they knew their manners and minded how they spoke. Not that she raised them soft. She knew that she'd do her kids no favours if her didn't give them a bit of backbone. Sometimes even now they tittered to themselves as to how they'd come running in blubbering after some kid had lamped them and how their mom had pushed them back outside with the words, 'Now goo and fight them and if y'come back blartin I'll give y'summat to really blart about!'

Then just as things had started to pick up for all of them, just as they'd started to earn a few bob and to buy her things and take her places, she was gone. They reproached themselves for not doing more, for not giving her everything she deserved. But in truth there was nothing to reproach themselves for. They'd given her all that she'd ever wanted. They'd given her the peace of mind that came from knowing her kids were alright and that her grandkids were on the way to really making something of themselves. That was all she wanted. Our Mom.

Vardos and Rais: The Romanies of the Black Patch

Long ago, the contaminated fumes of great manufacturing works had withered its grass, poisoned its waters and distorted its features. Hard on the borders of Winson Green, Handsworth and Smethwick, this rare piece of open ground had been seized upon as the miskin for nearby furnaces. Each day, carts filled with the stoney left-overs of still burning coal upturned their hot loads, leaving them to smoulder into masses of slag which rose up as if they were mountains of lava. Like a volcano-ravaged island, it worn't much of a spot. No wonder the local folk knew it only as the 'Black Patch.

Inhospitable and desolate, yes, but it was not empty and forlorn. For unattractive as it had become, this was the winter quarters of a hardy and determined group of Romany families. Though they were looked down on by many as 'gypos' and thieves, in common with most of their people, these Romanies were upright and honourable, hard-collaring and self-supporting. Pulled together by powerful bonds of blood, each summer they travelled into the rural West Midlands to pick peas and hops and do whatever task they could to scrat a living. Then as autumn fell, they harnessed their horses to their vardos – caravans – and headed back towards Brum and the part of the Black Patch between the railway line and Hockley Brook.

They'd been gathering there for at least 30 years when the 1900s woke and before that, they'd been based elsewhere in the locality. When they'd first arrived, their chavvies – children – had been able to run through green pastures and corn fields and gaze at the homes of wealthy men such as Edward Benson, the father of an Archbishop of Canterbury, and James Turner, the wealthy Brummagem button maker. But as the meadows had disappeared beneath houses and public buildings, the rich had fled and with no deeds or title, the Romanies could not gainsay the blemishing of the land they

The Romanies of the Black Patch in the late 1800s. Their king, Esau Smith, is holding the horse on the right, whilst standing at the back is his wife, Queen Henty, in her spotless white pinner and headscarf. The tunnel leads to Queen's Road and on to Handsworth. Thanks to Smethwick Local History Society.

thought their own and which no-one else cared for. Despite its soiling, they remained bound to the Black Patch and set their mark upon it. They had a 'Gypsy's Chapel' where they worshipped; they staked out portions to graze their horses; and between their caravans they set up cooking spaces, huts and wig wamish tents. Getting by through horse-trading, labouring, the hawking of clothes pegs and dukerin – fortune-telling – the Romanies had their own king who stepped in to stop any nonsense.

Esau Smith had been an eye-catching rai – young man – and even as an oldster, he drew attention with his white mutton chops, billycock, diklo (neckerchief) and dignified bearing. They reckoned he was one of the cutest judges of a horse in the country, and he was well respected by his people – the Smiths, Loveridges, Davises, Badgers and Claytons. When he died, aged 92 in 1901, he was laid out with pride in his caravan and his burial at Handsworth Old Church was attended by a great crowd of Romany mourners from near and far. Afterwards, his wife was declared Queen Henty and soon, she was beset by trials and tribulations.

The owners of the Black Patch wanted much of it for building and sought to shift the Romanies. Not surprisingly, these folk refused to abandon a plot which had been

Young Romanies on the Black Patch before their eviction. Notice the different types of caravan, the 'wig-wam' type tent in the middle and the tin bath in the foreground. Now living in Austria, George Smith comes from a Black Patch family. His father used to tell him 'about the riots which went on at the Black Patch until it came to the legendary battle for the area when the gipsies were ordered to leave for some reason.' George's grandfather, Tom Smith, even wrote to Buckingham Palace to complain about the eviction.

forsaken by all bar them. They had the moral right but not the legality and on July 27, 1905, they were evicted forcibly by a large force of sheriff's officers and policemen. The Romanies watched disconsolately as their carefully-cultivated potato patches were trodden over, their dwellings knocked down and their goods strewn under a railway arch. Angry men, wailing women and blarting babbies straggled off into the rain. Queen Henty and a few of the Smiths were allowed to remain. She died on January 7, 1907, and a week later, a pyre was made of her vardo and possessions. Within two years, the last of her people had been moved so that the Black Patch Park could be laid out. The Romanies of Old Brum were given little respect. It's not too late to give it to them now, for they too played their part in the making of Birmingham.

Black Patch Romany men. Amongst them are 18-year-old Bert 'Maize' Loveridge, seated on the right, and Dick Gordevoy on his left. Thanks to Don Loveridge. Don's brother, John, recalls that their dad, Maize, was born in a vardo going through Ludlow. He never went to school because he was too busy shusi (rabbit) hunting for food. Maize told his son that although they grafted picking fruit and hops, the Romanies were never welcome. When they'd finished their work and moved on, people would cry, 'Lock up your doors, here come the gypos!' No pub in Herefordshire or Worcestershire would let them in and Maize learned to be very hard, fighting those who insulted him and his people. His wife, Edith, wasn't a gypsy and her family disowned her. Now, John is proud to proclaim his Romany roots. After their removal from the Black Patch, Maize and his family lived in Winson Green Road near the families of his brother and sister and their father, Len, and his second wife, May. Jessie Loveridge is one of their children and recalls days when 'we were lucky to sit down to a real cooked meal'. Her dad used to walk to Hamstead Wood and Wasson Pool to collect herbs to make a tea.

Chapter 2:

The Old End

Down The Rock: Alum Rock

Which neighbourhood in Brum has the most intriguing name? Some might favour Druids Heath, thinking that it harks back to the days of the Celts and their white-robed priests, although actually its derived from the Drews, a family that farmed the land locally. Others might propose Soho, supposedly called after the cry of the hunters who once chased animals across that part of Handsworth Heath. And perhaps more could put forward Ninevah on the borders of Winson Green – bringing to mind the capital of the ancient Assyrians mentioned in the Bible.

There are plenty more mysterious-sounding Brummagem districts. What about California, Robin Hood and Rotton Park? Or Beggars Bush, Cockshut Hill and Dogpool? And let's not forget Alum Rock – where did that name come from? Some folks say it dates back to the early 1900s when Southalls, the big employer thereabouts, dug an artesian well and came across alum rock – a thin-bedded mineral from which comes a whitish mineral salt which is translucent. Certainly, as manufacturing chemists, the company may have found alum a useful raw material in some of their products if indeed they had come across it. But there's still a problem because the name of the area goes back at least to 1760 and that's 60 years before Southalls began business in Bull Street in the middle of Birmingham and way before they moved to Alum Rock.

That early evidence is shown on a map of Little Bromwich in the parish of Aston in the county of Warwick that was drawn by John Tomlinson. As well as Ward End Hall and Treford Hall he noted the Allum Rock Estate – bounded to the north by Slade Field and to the west by Brockhill, later known as Brookhill. So the puzzle remains; how did Alum Rock get its name, rooted so deep in our history as it is? Perhaps, the old stories are true, but instead of Southall's finding Alum Rock someone else did so over a century before. Whatever its origins, for many years Alum Rock was just a small locality, close to a stream known as the Wash Brook which divided Little Bromwich from Saltley. By the late 1800s it was still a rural spot with Alum Rock Farm on the Alum Rock Road itself, just south of the railway line and by the junction of what is today Sladefield Road, Pelham Road and Belchers Lane. Only a couple or three hundred yards away, back towards Brum, stood Alum Rock House and another prominent dwelling known as Fern Bank. That was about it, bar for a fulminate manufactory near to the present Rockville Road. And that raises more questions, for fulminate is any salt or ester of fulminic acid (an unstable and volatile acid), especially mercury salt, which is used as a detonator. So did this fulminate factory make detonators and who owned it?

Things stayed much the same as the twentieth century dawned, although a few shopkeepers opened up by the meeting point of the Alum Rock Road and Sladefield Road. And on the site of the fulminate works, Southall and Barclay built New Charnford Mills for the making of surgical dressings. But the district was soon to be transformed, as was made obvious in 1915 by the laying out of the Sutton Estate on Brook Hill. Paid for under the terms of the will of a wealthy London businessman, it had cracking houses on a smashing site on the slope leading down from Ward End Park and there were lovely views to the east where there were fields, market gardens and allotments.

That country feel soon disappeared, for within months of the end of the First World War, Birmingham City Council embarked on a policy of building great numbers of

ALUM ROCK RD   B.HAM.

The tram is coming up the Alum Rock road from Saltley, passing a horse and cart as it goes. It looks like the vehicle has just gone across the junctions of Bowyer Road, Gowan Road and Highfield Road. Hazel Hobday recalls that there used to be two shops here 'that always are clearly remembered. Jester's, a food store, on the junction of Gowan Road that has now been sealed off to the traffic, and the other known as the Corn Shop. They sold pet foods, vegetables, fruit, seeds, not to mention the corn that the man used to throw out to feed the pigeons.' Further up the Rock, up by Southall's, was a bicycle shop 'where an old man sat inside repairing bikes. In his window he used to have two pictures showing the Alum Rock Road and Cotterill's Lane with just trees lining the roads.

corporation houses – homes fit for heroes. There's no doubt that they were badly needed. Almost 200,000 Brummies lived in out-of-date, insanitary back to-backs which couldn't be cleared until modern homes were ready. Alum Rock was a prime site for development. Adjoining the built-up area of Saltley to the west and with a main route running through it, the area was mostly open land well suited for building upon. From 1919 one of Brum's first large-scale council estates stretched outwards to the

Despatching goods from Southalls in the 1920s. Thanks to Smith and Nephew. The front of the building looks much the same today. Southall's was and is a major employer locally and Rose Davis, née Edwards, recalls that there used to be a bit of a dance opposite the works which was called the 'Arcadia'. Colin Draper was born nearby at 75, Couchman Road – which was also 75, Parkfield Road. This was because the building was a corner shop owned by Colin's Gran, Alice Roberts. Two year later, Colin's family moved further up the Rock to a brand new house at 42, Bankdale Road. Colin and his brothers, Bryan and Keith, atttended what was then Alum Rock Road School, now Anthony Road School.

Shirley Goodwin grew up in Hartopp Road, next door to where her father had been born in a house which remained the family home until the death of his last sister, who never married. She brings to mind the shop of Mrs Eagles, on the corner of Hartopp and College Roads and Joan's the hairdressers on the opposite corner. Next door was Chapman's TV repair shop, whilst King's, a family removal firm, was at the top of College Road. Also in that road were Kutes the newsagents together with the 'best' fish and chip shop beside the alley which led to the College Road Assembly Rooms. Opposite was the pawn shop complete with the three-ball symbol. The Co-operative Society also had a grocery store on the corner of College and Couchman Roads.

River Cole and Stechford and downwards to Bordesley Green East and the Fever Hospital. Focused on Cotterills Lane, it boasted good-quality parlour-type houses, each of which had dressers, cupboards, gas lighting, scullery, three bedrooms and a separate bathroom. Arguably, with those erected at Billesley, Pineapple Farm and Stonehouse, they were the best corporation dwellings constructed in Birmingham during the interwar years.

The rapid growth of population soon led to clusters of shops appearing by two pubs, the 'Pelham' and the 'Brookhill'. But there was little doubt that the most important shopping centre was the 'Rock' itself. In fact this important road led to the name Alum Rock spreading to take in much of Saltley, up past Shaw Hill and as far as Bowyer Road and Highfield Road. Alum Rock remains a vibrant district. It might have a quizzical name, but no-one can ignore its significance to modern Brum.

This is a photograph of Charlie Smith holding the bridle of a shire horse in Couchman Road, Alum Rock in 1927. Charlie used to live in Woodbine Cottage and when the cottage was demolished to make way for the Morris Commercial Club, he moved into a house opposite his old home. Charlie's Dad had a successful delivery business based on fourteen shire horses and later switched to motorised transport. Charlie still lives locally. Thanks to Charlie Smith and Roy and Christine Hewitt.

Alum Rock itself ws developed slowly from the later 1800s and Jill Herdman's great grandparents, the Smiths, once farmed the land which was to be covered by privately-bought terraced housing in the Parkfield Road, Anthony Road and Ludlow Road neighbourhood in the later years of the nineteenth century and the early twentieth century. She still has the bill of sale for the farm amounting to £300. It covered a big house, outhouses, carts, horses and all the farm implements down to the nails. The urbanisation of Alum Rock was not completed until the inter-war years with the building of the large Cotterills Lane council estate.

Fields and Picture Houses: Birchfield

The 'Odeon Theatre' on the Birchfield Road was the most beautiful and amazing picture house that anyone had ever been in. In fact it was more than a picture house, for the very name itself was infused with sensations of luxury and quality and stood in sharp contrast to the more down-to-earth buildings which normally showed films. What did the word Odeon actually stand for? Well, some said it was Greek and others stated its letters were an acronym for a slogan which brought to mind the man whose great concept this was: Oscar Deutsch Entertains Our Nation. Whatever it meant, it didn't really matter for as you tried the name on your tongue it seemed to send your mind soaring into make believe worlds and dream palaces.

Oscar Deutsch himself was a Brummie Jew whose family was involved with the Brenners in running a metal, skin and waste rubber merchants in Harford Street. But Oscar had not been drawn into that concern. Instead he had been pulled into the film business and had set his sights on showing pictures in the most eye-catching and exotic of theatres. The 'Odeon' on the Birchfield Road was the realisation of his dreams. Located between Canterbury Road and Thornbury Road, it was built by B. Whitehouse and Sons Ltd of Monument Road and it could accommodate the great number of 1,820 people. Prices ranged from just a tanner to one and thrupence and patrons were entertained not only by the films but also by a fine seventeen-piece orchestra.

The 'Odeon Theatre' in Birchfield was the first Odeon to be built in the country and it took the name of the district around the city and, indeed, further afield. Today, however, few people identify the area and it seems in danger of fading into history. Locally, many people declare that they live in Perry Barr or Handsworth, and apart from the Birchfield Road itself and the odd signpost, there is little to bring Birchfield to the fore. Yet, like Ashted, Gosta Green, Spring Hill, Duddeston, Springfield and other old Brummagem neighbourhoods, Birchfield should not be allowed to drift from consciousness.

As its name suggests, the locality recalls the birch trees which once were noticeable in its fields and for centuries it was one of the hamlets of Handsworth. The urbanisation of Birchfield came late, beginning only in the mid-nineteenth century, and was signalled by the consecration of the Church of Holy Trinity on Whit Tuesday May 17, 1864. Its architect was the celebrated Julius Alfred Chatwin, who designed, restored or enlarged more than 30 churches in the Birmingham district. A year later, Holy Trinity became a parish in its own right, so giving a focus to the emerging suburb of Birchfield, and in 1869 a church school was opened in Finch Road – later transferred to Wilson Road.

By the 1890s, a large number of grand houses were obvious in the vicinity of the church and there was a sizeable open space owned by the Excelsior Cricket Club. This sports ground disappeared in the early twentieth century with the cutting of Freer Road and by this date the district to the north of Trinity Road and between the Birchfield Road and Witton Road had been covered with good quality houses for the lower middle class. As in Bournbrook, many of the roads brought to mind the West Country, such as Tintern Road – or else they recalled names in the south of England, as with Bayswater Road, and in northern France, as with Normandy Road.

On its east side, Aston side, shops lined the Birchfield Road from its beginnings at the Aldridge Road down to Thornbury Road. Thanks to Johnny Landon. Further along, another stretch of retailers began at Fentham Road and went to Six Ways, Aston. Amongst them was Jolly's Radio Shop, which at 71, Birchfield Road stood betwen Mansfield Road and Fentham Road. Emma Bygrave remembers that the business started round the corner from Witton Road in Aston Lane and that Mr Jolly used to buy his goods from her father-in-law, William Bygrave of Constitution Hill.

To the left of Jolly's is a jewellery shop which was run by Hazel Bryan and her husband. They had the premises from just after the Second World War until they left the Midlands to move to Devon in 1959. Before the war, Hazel lived in Earlsbury Gardens and her husband to be in Hatfield Road, and after their wedding they moved to Perry Barr, close to the Birchfield Harriers ground. This photograph also shows Sharma's oriental and continental grocery, which indicates the immigration of South Asian people to Birchfield. Previously, these premises had been a cafe run by Derian Said and in the 1940s it had been a tobacconist occupied by Harry Flavell. Indeed, as far back as 1911, it had specialised in selling tobacco, then under William Wasdale Holltum. The shop to the left of Jolly's was that of John W. Bryan, clock and watch repairers. Fifty years before, Harry Kelland had been there as a watch repairer. These buildings disappeared in the redevelopments of 1960s Birmingham.

Although many people called it the 'Odeon' Perry Barr, the first Odeon was at Birchfield. This photograph emphasises the eye-catching design of a building which was to become the prototype for Odeons elsewhere in Britain. Mrs M. Pickett, née Vernon, explains that in the early days of the Second World War it was realised that the whiteness of the 'Odeon' would cause it to be a landmark for German bombers. As a result it was bricked in.

Before he was called up during the war, Marjorie K. Sutton's husband used to work for the Swish Curtain Rail Company which was 'not far from his home in Clement Street off the Parade .... and when the 'Odeon' Picture House was being built in Birchfield Road his firm got an order for rail, and he was the delivery boy at the time. So with the long lengths of rail tied on to an old bike, he navigated the roads to the 'Odeon' safely. What he did not know or notice was that a man had just completed an area of concrete in front of the steps leading to the main doors: 'He dropped his old bike, untied the rails and trailed right across the poor man's work. He didn't know which was worse – the man's anger or fear of the sack if reported. However he survived both and said this was his claim to fame, footprints in the concrete.'

Laurence Burton saw many films at the 'Odeon', 'where it was one shilling and threepence for a front stall seat and one and ninepence in the rear stalls, elevated above the front, and two shillings and threepnce in the balcony. The programmes were continous, not necessarily at set times, and you might take your seat in the middle of a film and then sit and see it through and round to that point before leaving'. The 'Odeon' provided 'our only visual perception of news and current affairs through the agencies of Pathe and Movietone and also there were forerunners of commercial advertising in which short clips of promoting the film were shown during intervals between the main performances.' A special feature of the 'Odeon' was the manager himself who was resplendent in dinner jacket and black bow tie and who stood in the foyer, 'flower button hole in place, whilst the customers passed through – wielding the power of his small entertainment kingdom (and didn't he do well!).'

Locally, the facilities were mostly developed by the Handsworth Urban District Council. In 1895, the Birchfield Road Board School was opened for 660 pupils, whilst in 1907 Canterbury Road School was built. The rapid rise in population of Birchfield was emphasised by the fact that this last school could hold 1,220 infants and juniors. Like the rest of Handsworth, Birchfield became part of Birmingham in 1911 – but even by then the survival of the district name was in danger. This was because back in 1837 a railway station had opened by the 'Crown and Cushion'. Although it was south of the River Tame and in Birchfield it was actually called 'Perry Barr'. Mind you, the name of Birchfield does live on strongly with the success of an internationally-known organisation – that of Birchfield Harriers. Formed in 1877, its athletes have taken the name of Birchfield across the world and into the Olympics. It's not a bad boast for a place that it was the site of the first Odeon in Brum and that it gave its name to a cracking athletics club. Birchfield should live on.

Taken on 27 March, 1962, this shot of the newly-opened underpass at Birchfield shows how this wide road has cut a swathe through the neighbourhood. Thanks to the Birmingham <u>Evening Mail</u>. Crowds have gathered to see the official car pass underneath. On the right can be seen the 'Birchfield Picture House' between Bragg Road and Aston Lane. Opened as the 'Birchfield Picturedome' on Thursday October 16, 1913, it seated 900 people and prices were 3d and 6d with a high of 9d in the Grand Balcony. It was built by the noted firm of Elvins and Son at a cost of £4,530. That year Elvins also constructed the 'Springfield Picture Playhouse' on the Stratford Road, Springfield for £3,297 and the 'Paramount Picture Theatre', Cannock for £1,961. A year before, Elvins had built their first cinema, the Great Hampton Street Picture Palace, for the sum of £2,124. The 'Birchfield' itself closed on March 3, 1962 when it was showing 'South Pacific'.

Barbara Csepreghy has always lived in the Perry Barr/Great Barr area and has many memories of Birchfield which is just down the road. She tells me that the University of Central England occupies part of the site of the old Birchfield Road School and that the Saint John's Church Vicarage was further along, whilst the church itself was in the aptly-named Church Road. In her youth, Barbara was secretary to Leslie Dyer-Smith, a chartered accountant in Colmore Row who was also secretary for the 'Birchfield Picture House', 'and I remember going there from school in 1951, one Christmas, to see "Scrooge" (or "A Christmas Carol") and it was Alastair Sim as Scrooge. It scared us all half to death, black and white film, lights out on the stairs when we came down to go home and snowing outside!' Barbara herself went to Canterbury Road School and had a lovely headmistress called Miss Baggs. She also recalls the traffic jams by the old 'Crown and Cushion' pub, which had a big frontage.

Ted Edgar explains that the 'Birchfield' was not on such a grand scale as the 'Odeon', 'but nevertheless it was a nice little friendly place. The only drawback was that if you had to queue it was outside under a corrugated roof – alright in the summer and it kept the chill winds off you, but if it rained, my God you could hardly hear yourself speak for the rain hammering on the corrugated sheets. This was the cinema where I first saw Cinemascope – widescreen – with 'The Robe'.'

Lords, Gaffers and Workers: Cardigan Street

Brummagem in the 1800s was celebrated as a big town packed full with little gaffers – a place where every man Jack felt he was as good as the next feller. More than that, it was renowned as a centre of those who believed that hard work and not inherited wealth should be the key to a person's success. Yet for all its people's attachment to egalitarianism, much of Brum was possessed by titled families who gained their income not through manufacturing but from renting. So, which area has the most noble connections?

Some might plump for Edgbaston, cut through with roads denoting the ownership of the barons Gough-Calthorpe of Norfolk. Others might put forward Highgate, much of which belonged to Sir Thomas Gooch, whose seat was Benacre Hall in the Suffolk village of Wrentham. Still more might propose Saltley, where Ralph, Edmund and Reginald Roads recall members of the Adderley family, the Lords Norton. There are other claimants, for if Aston is linked to the descendants of Sir Thomas Holte then Small Heath is bonded to the barons Digby of Tilton Hall in Leicestershire.

But for all these lordly associations, few parts of Birmingham can match the Cardigan Street neighbourhood for its aristocratic ties. Small and oblongish, it is squashed between Ashted to the east, Gosta Green to the north, the off-lying streets of Digbeth to the west and the wide expanse of rail lines running to Curzon Street Station to the south. For centuries this district was part of Duddeston in the parish of Aston, only joining Brum in 1838 – by which date its relationship to land-owning families was well established.

The eastern boundary of the Cardigan Street neighbourhood is Lawley Street, called after Sir Robert Lawley, MP for North Warwickshire in the 1780s and a supporter of the General Hospital and other charities; whilst its southern limit recalls the Curzons. They gained their property locally after the death in 1798 of William Jennens, a fabulously wealthy bachelor. The last of a line which originally had made its money from the iron trade in Birmingham, Jennens did not make a will and much of his estate was passed on to Lady Sophia Howe – hence Howe Street. She was the eldest daughter of Admiral Howe who had defeated the French in a major battle in the North Atlantic in 1794. News of this victory reached Birmingham on the day of the town's fair and was greeted with 'the ringing of the bells, and firing of the guns, united with the exulting exclamations of innumerable voices in our crowded streets'. Lady Sophia married the Honourable Penn Assheton Curzon, who is brought to mind in Penn Street as well as Curzon Street. Similarly, Cardigan Street relates to Harriett Georgina Bridinell, the sister to the 6th Earl of Cardigan who led the Charge of the Light Brigade and gave his name to a piece of clothing.

Harriet's husband was Richard William Penn. Later becoming Earl Howe, he laid the foundations of the Queen's Hospital in Bath Row (afterwards the Acci) in 1840 and lived in grandeur at Gopsal Hall in Leicestershire – the origins of Gopsal Street. Yet if the streets of the Cardigan Street neighbourhood hark of the landed elite, then the district was filled with hard-collaring, working-class Brummies living mostly in back-to-backs. Grafting at firms like Holder's Brewery in Nova Scotia Street, they sent their kids to Fox Street School, later known as Grosvenor Street School; they worshipped at the Wesleyan Belmont Row Chapel and at St. Peter's Mission in Cardigan Street; they relaxed in the 'Railway' on the corner of Howe Street and the 'King's Arms' in Prince's Row; and they shopped with the likes of Mrs Chattaway of Cardigan Street, whose huckster's doubled up as a coffee house.

Miss Alice Wilcox's shop on the corner of Howe Steet and Curzon Street, 1930s Sheila Knight, née Hodgkiss, lived at 2 back of 30 Gopsal Street, where the bedroom at the back of the house was used only for storage because it overlooked Whittaker Ellis's yard 'and the smell of oil and petrol was dreadful'. This house was also next door to the pig and rubbish bins and the three outside toilets that served the yard. The resultant mixed smells, mice and sticky fly papers filled with dead flies 'sounds like a recipe for disaster, but no. Our house was full of love and warmth. Mom made sure it was spotless, the window-sill and the step gleamed red from cardinal polish, as did the floor in the front room and the small kitchen.'

Sheila and the other local children played freely and often would go off to lark about on the bombed site down Curzon Street which was known as The Peck. The families in the yard were good friends and everyone helped each other and Sheila is still in touch with the wonderful Lacey family. She and hers sisters and their families have done well and 'I feel sure that both parents would be justly proud of their family and, maybe the humble years spent in Gopsal Street taught us morals, manners and a strong will to survive'.

The guts and determination of the local folk were epitomised by Winifred Yate of Gopsal Street. During the Blitz, she helped lead 200 heavy, dray horses from the stables of the Co-op in Belmont Row and which adjoined burning premises. One animal stepped on her foot and injured it, but Winifred remained on duty until the all clear sounded. A few days later, the brave Brummie rescued two men hurt by falling debris during an air raid, after which an explosion injured her so badly that she had to spend three months in hospital. Little wonder that Winifred was honoured with the British Empire Medal. Soon Millennium Point will dominate the Cardigan Street neighbourhood. Would it not be fitting to have a plaque recalling the bravery of Winifred Yate and would it not be meet to have a mural depicting the lives of those who once lived locally?

Here's Penn Street all decked out for a Coronation Day street party in 1953. The 'Eagle and Ball' is the pub in the background, on the corner of Gopsal Street. Thanks to Mrs Dorothy McEvoy, née Latham. Dorothy was born at 9, Penn Street and stresses the high number of little factories locally, such as Armstrong's Metal Works, the Transport Seating Company and the Stag Display Company. This last was 'well liked in the area. It held such a fascination to the local children as they made all the display lights for illuminations and commercial use. They trimmed up our local streets for Coronation really professionally.'

Steve Edmonds is second from the right at the back and in the middle of the doorway in this photo he sent in of seven-year olds at Grosvenor Street School in 1932. The female teacher was Miss Taylor and Steve recalls that amongst the children were Bob Barber, Paddy Whelan, Bob Munday, Alf Batchelor and Ernie Guest. Steve lived at 12, Cardigan Street until July 27, 1942, when a bomb dropped on the family's house, and he worked in the street at J. and H. Engineering – which repaired all types of machines.

There was plenty of work locally. From AB Row into Cardigan Street, on the right-hand side, was Thomas Merry, the paint manufacturer, then Goff the cardboard box maker and Jennings and Son who were draughtsmen – behind which was J. and H. Engineering. Going on down was a small coalyard belonging to Mrs Broadhurst, Mr Smart's sweet shop and grocery store (which also had two one-armed bandit machines), Goff's main office and works, and Mrs Moore's sweet shop. On the other side of the street was a boarding house, Mrs Clay's sweet shop (her son became the chief fire officer and her grandson owned the music shop in Broad Street) and Whittaker Ellis, the gas contractors. This latter place employed most of the local men, including Steve's Dad who was a gangerman.

Stan Pratt was born in Cardigan Street in 1927. His mom and dad were the caretakers at the premises of Whittaker Ellis Ltd, the engineering contractors for public works, whilst his dad was also a bummer – foreman – for the firm.

At that time the men had to pull a cart 'with all the gear on sometimes as far out as Coleshill. It was hard work in them days,' and as a lad Stan used to go with his dad and the men to make the tea for them. He well remembers Mrs Chattaway and Mrs Clay who kept shops in Cardigan Street, the 'King's Arms' in Howe Street, now a cafe, and the 'Eagle and Ball' in Gopsal Street, today 'Murphy's Bar'.

James Waldron's maternal grandad was also a caretaker at Whittaker Ellis and the family held all their parties in the works' canteen. More than that, James's dad was another one of Whittaker Ellis's employees, laying gas pipes and repairing leaks. The family lived in Cardigan Street and then Gopsal Street and James has fond memories of visits to the ice cream shop of the Iommis in nearby Buck Street. The Italian Brummies also had a greengrocer's on the corner of Cardigan and Gopsal Streets, whilst on Coleshill Street was a music shop run by the well-known Tamburros.

Homes and Town Planning: Harborne Ideal Tenants

J.S. Nettlefold was one of the most energetic figures in the political life of Birmingham at the dawn of the twentieth century. A member of the great manufacturing family which gave its name to Guest, Keen and Nettlefold, he was a prominent Liberal Unionist, a firm supporter of Joseph Chamberlain and in 1901 he became chairman of the newly-formed Housing Committee on the Council. The greatest problem facing Nettlefold was that of slum housing. Birmingham had over 40,000 badly-built and insanitary back-to-backs and a wide range of reports made it clear that such dwellings were life threatening and injurious to health. Both Socialists and Radical Conservatives believed that the only way to clear Brum of this problem was to embark on a widespread policy of slum clearance and council house building. Nettlefold set himself against this plan. A passionate supporter of the free market, he believed firmly that the problem of slum housing could be solved by the efforts of private enterprise.

Folk milling about looking at the completed houses on the Harborne Tenants Estate at the opening ceremony, May 24, 1908. A year after this event, Mrs Cecily Eden was born in Moorpool Avenue, the main through road on the Harborne Tenants Estate. The garden hedges were beech and in part there were hedges of wild roses in Carter's Avenue. Cecily notes that unique feature of the design of the dwellings is that there is a winding passage at the side and back of each house, adjacent to which are the allotments. Then as now, the circle was the hub of social life and Cecily's father helped to found the chess club, whilst Sunday School classes were held in the hall. During the First World War, a Co-op shop traded beside the Post Office, and 'probably the very active Co-op Guild women had their meeting above the shop'. A group of Belgian refugees was given refuge in a Moorpool Avenue house. All these years later, Cecily explains that 'the tranquil little Moorpool looks to me just as it did'.

The 'Olde Englishe Festival' on the Harborne Tenants Estate, May 1909. The first May Queen locally was May Connolly. Indeed the Connolly/Clarkson family are believed to be the oldest Catholic family in Harborne and May's father, Thomas Andrew Connolly, was the first foreman painter on the estate. James S. Kendall was also born on the Harborne Tenants Estate, in his case in 1921, and he lived there in the main until he married in 1947. In his childhood and youth, it was a rare thing to see a motor car locally and deliveries were by horse cart. In particular, James recalls Johnny Evans, known as 'Old Shouty, and his vegetable cart and the man who measured milk from the churn and into the jug'. After he was invalided out of the army in 1941, following six months in hospital due to enemy action, James immediately joined the Home Guard, 21st Battalion, D Company Signals at Moorpool Hall.

Nettlefold argued that the prosperous members of the working class would move into good quality and newly-constructed dwellings and thus the poor would be able to rent the homes which had been vacated. In this way the back-to-backs of the city would come to be abandoned. Many people declared that such a policy was unworkable. The poor would not be able to afford the rents of the houses of the upper working class – and anyway such homes were in the suburbs and thus were away from the sources of cheap food and casual employment upon which the poor depended. Nettleford ignored such criticism and steadfastly adopted an approach which was derided as slum patching. He authorised the limited and piecemeal demolition of the worst dwellings and served notices on the owners of badly maintained homes to improve their properties. In particular, he gave his name to Nettlefold Courts – those yards which were opened up to light and fresh air through the knocking down of the two houses which fronted on to the street.

Yet if Nettlefold could be criticised for his approach to the problem of the back-to-backs, he was a man to be praised both for his forward-thinking attitude towards town planning and the expansion of Birmingham so as to incorporate places such as Kings Norton, Northfield, Yardley, Erdington and Handsworth. Encouraged by developments in Germany and at Bournville, Nettlefold enthusiastically explained that it was necessary to prevent the emergence of new slums in the suburbs through the adoption of clear town planning principles. At the same time, Birmingham had to expand to take in rural areas so as to enable the building of estates in which there was space, greenery and well-designed houses and roads.

Nettlefold lost the chairmanship of the Housing Committee in 1909 and two years later he failed to be re-elected as a councillor. Still, his principles of sound town planning were put into action and remain obvious in the Birmingham of the early twenty-first century. But he did not shrink from public life and remained deeply

Members of the Moorpool Tennis Club in 1960, with thanks to Mabel Utting. Mabel lived on the Harborne Tenants Estate for 30 years, having a shop on the Circle called 'Mabs' where she did sewing, pearl threading, tailoring and laundry and acted as a shoe repairs agent: 'I always had a chair in the shop for first comers to rest, and would provide many of them with cups of tea. I also sold ladies dresses and haberdashery, wool and baby clothes'. Mabel's home was on East Pathway, opposite the Green, 'where the old maypole used to be set up', and she used to rent an allotment on the estate. She was also a founder member of the Circle Players, 'a company which stages its plays at Moorpool Hall', and along with her husband she was a member of both the tennis and bowling clubs.

involved in the affair of Birmingham. In 1907 he had become chairman of the Harborne Tenants Limited, and imbued with Nettlefold's beliefs, this body sought to build a garden suburb in Harborne. The aim was to show that it was possible to erect sound houses which would be let at reasonable rents and still show a profit for investors. Importantly, the new estate would be based on co-operative ownership and administration so that 'the interests of the tenant and of the investor are harmonised by an equitable division of the profits, and the consequent additional care bestowed upon the property by the tenants'.

Aiming to bring together tenant and capitalist in mutual support, the Harborne Tenants took an option held by Nettlefold on 36 acres of land between Lordswood, Ravenhurst and Wentworth Roads in Harborne. Costing £15,860, the estate ultimately contained 54 acres of undulating land close to Harborne Station and was in a district which was one of the healthiest parts of Birmingham. Suitably, Mrs Nettlefold cut the first sod of the development on October 26, 1907. She declared that soon the estate would boast well laid-out houses, nice spaces, grass and trees and that there would be space for recreation and for the children to play in. Heavy traffic was not anticipated but the roads would be narrow to discourage vehicles and to allow more space for the houses.

By September 1908, 14 houses had been completed, 40 were nearing completion and were let and 25 more were in the process of construction. The aim was to build 500 homes by 1912 and so that the garden suburb idea might be allowed to flourish, every tree on the estate was kept whilst new trees and shrubs were planted. Nettlefold may have been wrong in setting his face against council house building but the continuing success of the Harborne Tenants Estate emphasise that he was a visionary in the field of town planning and the provision of good houses. As he explained, housing had to be made to pay yet it was 'no good building castles unless people can afford to live in them'.

Traipsing in Fields: Highgate

It was a cracking summer's day in the late 1700s, so off they traipsed down Cheapside – a street freshly cut out of fields – and into the countryside. Above them stood Lombard House, close to where Ravenshurst Street would later start. A large rural residence, it overlooked the 'Apollo' Hotel, just across the River Rea and at the bottom of Moseley Street. They were tempted to stop and have tea in the gardens of the pub, but they decided to head on for Vaughton's Hole, where Vaughton Street now joins Gooch Street. It was a smashing day for a swim and that pool was the best place locally for a dip. Mind you, they didn't all go in at the same time. One of them watched over their clothes, for the last time they'd been there they'd been skylarking and someone had pinched a fob watch.

After their swim they dried out and crossed the weak Rea where a few large stones had been chucked in. Then they struck up towards the Deritend Brewery at the junction of Moseley Street and Alcester Street. Carrying on, they reached the top of Camp Hill and sat down by Stratford House, the home of the Simcox family since 1691 and the centre of a farm of twenty acres. Soon enough they were off again and after a few yards they reached the toll gate on the turnpike rod to Alcester, situated at the top end of

Wearing the white hat and sitting next to the coachman is George Carter, the licensee of the 'White Swan' on the corner of Moseley Street and Lombard Street, probably just before 1914. George is taking his customers on a trip to the Stratford Mop. Not long after this, George died and later his widow remarried to a Joseph Cox, who was the grandfather known by Graham Edwards who sent in this picture.

Skirts Lane or Kyrwicks Lane as it would be called later. At this high gate, they halted to draw in the view. And what a smashing view it was! Staring ahead, they gazed over the fields of Highgate where rabbits (coneys) ran in the barley (bere), the origin of Conybere Street. Below that spot they saw the white cottage of Longmoors Farm. Owned by the Cox family, the estate stretched from just past Vaughton's Hole into Balsall Heath. On the other side of the Rea, they could see both Bell Barn and Windmill Farms on the slopes of Holloway Head. Then turning their heads to the right they took in the way in which Brummagem was seeking out fields to cover with houses, shops and factories. But the thing that really captured their eyes was the church of St Martin's in the Bull Ring.

A smashing shot looking down Emily Street from Dymoke Street, 1930s. This photograph was taken shortly before this end of Emily Street was cleared to make way for the St Martin's Flats which were completed by 1939.

Trudy Taylor's Highgate memories are of her father's pet shop in Vaughton Street, which he took over about 1929. He sold birds and small pets, importing the birds from Holland until the mid 1930s when the Wild Birds Act came about. After that he sold pigeons. His name was Harry Hunt and his shop was known to fanciers all over the Midlands, in fact it became an unofficial club. Trudie recalls that 'buying a bird was not to be taken lightly. It was inspected, handled and talked about between them all.'

Len Baron was born in that part of Dymoke Street which lay between Angelina and Conybere Streets. There were plenty of shops, locally, like that of Mrs Mayhew whose premises 'were packed to bursting point. She sold everything from sweets to collar studs, and hair pins to a bag of flour or a loaf of bread.' Then there was Mrs Phillips who owned the tripe shop and also cooked chitterlings and faggots and 'piping hot peas, which I am sure graced many a table for Friday night's tea'. Nearby was a small sweet and bread shop run by Kate Bowel and her brother, 'most obliging characters,' and further along was Mrs James's coalyard. And on the corner with Angelina Street was the 'pop shop', pawn shop of Mrs Giles.

They were getting parched and clammed now, but relief was nearby. One more push and they were at the 'Orange Tree' public house, close to where Highgate Square would emerge. Built in 1780, it was a popular resort for the many folk who rambled through the countryside of Highgate on Sundays. After a game of bowls on the green,

Two lads staring at the camera in Angelina Street in 1965. Thanks to Johnny Landon. Mrs J. M. Sutton recalls that this was a second-hand shop on the corner of Vaughton Street and that it was run by a lady called Ada Berrows. Three weeks after Mrs Sutton moved into nearby Leopold Street, she had a son and she bought a pram off Ada for seven shillings. R. Berrow is one of the seven children of Mrs Berrow, who was also known as Mrs Fox, so that she had 'three Berrows and four Foxes'. It seemed that the whole of the district passed through the shop 'because there was as much bought as there was sold. People sold when they were broke and needed ready cash and bought when they were more flush'. Amongst the goods traded were old-fashioned whale bone stays, second-hand shoes, carpets, beds, stoves, sewing machines and much more. Ada also worked in the Rag Alley in the Bull Ring and at Bilston Market every Monday, where, R. Berrow relates, 'she was a greater character than in Brum. She could speak in a broad Black Country accent and they would not believe she was bred and born in Brum'.

Lyn Swadkins was born at 92, Angelina Street in 1944 and her dad, Tom Barfield, had the fishing tackle shop to the left of Mrs Berrows's shop. Tom had the business from the early 1950s until the mid-1960s when the building was knocked down. He used to make and repair fishing rods and was self taught. Of such a high quality were his goods that men would come to him from all over the Midlands.

they headed off home, but not before taking in the imposing Highgate House of Henry Haden, the button maker. Located at the present-day junction of Belgrave Road and the Moseley Road, it was a large structure set in 22 acres of land.

Highgate continued to pull in Brummie day trippers well into the 1800s, but the reach of Birmingham was ever longer and the onset of urbanisation was heralded in the late 1830s when Haden's Estate was developed and Belgrave Street (later road) emerged. Within 30 years, most of the rest of Highgate was overlain with streets many of which carried male and female names probably connected to the Macdonald family: Adelaide, Angelina, Charles Henry, Emily, Frank, Leopold and William Edward. And then there were the surnames recalled in Dymoke, Hick and Stanhope Streets.

Swiftly a vital, new working-class neighbourhood grew up, but one spot remained rural. It was a swathe of pasture left to trustees in 1790 by the will of Elizabeth Hollis so that an income might provide clothing for poor people in Birmingham and Aston. The land was at the highest point on the south of Birmingham and when it was found that the trustees wanted to sell it for building, the council put pressure on until it was able to buy the plot in 1876. On part of it was erected Chandos Road School, but the rest was laid out as Highgate Park. It's there that you can draw in still the days when walkers roamed the fields of Highgate.

Roman Roads and Making Things: Icknield Street

It's funny to think that some of the earliest people who lived in the Birmingham area were Roman soldiers. But that's certainly the case, for the Romans have left a tantalising trace of their presence at Metchley Park in Edgbaston. In his history of Birmingham written in the late 1700s, William Hutton described the place as 'The Camp'. It was a fortification which covered about 30 acres and although in many parts it had been levelled by farmers, 'pieces of armour are frequently ploughed up, particularly parts of the sword and the battle-axe'.

The base had been set up about 50 AD as part of the Roman campaign against the Celtic king Caratacus, which led to the conquest of the west Midlands. With a break or two, soldiers were maintained at Metchley for another 50 years. Unfortunately, much of the evidence for the Roman occupation was lost because of building work for the local canal and railway and for the Queen Elizabeth Hospital. Metchley had been chosen as a site because it lay on a major military route constructed by the Romans. This was Icknield Street, which ran from Bourton on the Water in the Cotswolds to Templeborough near Rotherham in Yorkshire. On its way, it went through Alcester, Wall, Little Chester and Chesterfield, as well as Birmingham.

Bert Garradley's earliest recollection of Icknield Street was of its 'bustling daily activity'. The family's house fronted on to the street and was directly opposite Lodge Road and a few yards away from Key Hill. The traffic here 'was to me, both as a junior and senior schoolboy, a constant source of wonderment and trepidation. The awe-inspiring spectacle of its diversity and the fear induced by its hazards aroused in me an excitement that I have never forgotten.' In particular, Bert recalls the horse-drawn vehicles of the Great Western Railway, Scribbans bakers' vans, R. White's mineral water carts and the Atora Beef Suet wagons drawn by bullocks. This photo shows Bert's Mom, May Garradley, standing in the front doorway of her house at 63, Icknield Street with four of her grandchildren. Allan is on the left with his younger sister, and on the right are Bert Garradley's younger sister's two children.

The road shares its name with the Icknield Way, a prehistoric trackway which went from The Wash to Dorset. No-one knows the meaning of the word and to make matters even more puzzling, Icknield Street is also known as Ricknield Street. This name came about in the Middle Ages when folk talked of 'at there Icknilde strete.' Gradually the 'r' from 'there' became detached and instead was latched on to the front of Icknield, so that people said 'at the Ricknilde strete.'

·Reaching Brum from Beoley, Icknield Street went by way of Lifford Lane in Kings Norton, the Pershore Road in Stirchley, Great Hampton Street in Hockley, Wellhead Lane in Perry Barr and into Sutton Park – thus leading to Streetly, the clearing by the street. Whether it actually ever went along our own Icknield Street is difficult to determine, although nineteenth-century Brummies believed this to be the case. They felt that from Metchley Park, the street eventually went into Monument Lane, and, of course, this road stops at Spring Hill and Summer Hill – across which Icknield Street begins.

'The Warstone' pub stood on the corner of Icknield Street and Camden Street and it was where Alan and Sheila Blaney met in 1959. Thanks to John Landon. The gaffer was Bert Chalk and he and his wife had two daughters – Margaret and Mary. Sheila recollects that 'it was a nice pub where you could take a friend' and it was nice and clean. Bert used to sing on Saturday or Sunday nights. He had a lovely voice and would sing 'Mother of Mine' and 'We three little lambs who have lost our way'. Then there was a chap called Stan Gibbs who played the piano and Johnny Baldwin who played the spoons. After the Chalks left to take over the 'Star' at Aston Cross, a young couple called Doug and Barbara took over 'The Warstone'. Sheila herself is from King Edwards Road and her Mom, Lily Mitchell, had a grocer's shop. Alan came out of Spring Hill and his dad was a chimney sweep. The two of them were married at Saint Paul's, Hockley in 1961 and they held their reception at the 'Warstone', as they had their engagement party.

Although bonded to so old a way, the Brummagem Icknield Street doesn't seem to have appeared until the early nineteenth century when it was shown on Kempson's Map (1808) as Ladywood Lane. It started at Summer Hill, where there was a toll gate on the Turnpike Road to Dudley, and it went on to Forest's Brewery on the corner of

Nobby Jones, who sent in this photo, is the lad in the front with the ball in the picture of the football team at Icknield Street School taken about 1948 in the playground. Nobby used to live at 10 Icknield Street.

A famous former resident of Icknield Street is Gladys Morgan, who as Lisbeth Kearns (after her marriage, Lisa Daniels) became a film star and whose family ran a fish and chip shop in Icknield Street. Her sister, Edna Boaz, writes that the family took over the business in 1929 and lived there for 43 years. Their mother, May, won £100 on a News of the World *competition and moved from Wales to the fish and chip shop. It was a hard life and 'Mom used to push a large basket on small wheels six days a week to the wholesale fish market in Bell Street at 5 o'clock in the morning'. Edna and Gladys both went to Ellen Street School and Camden Street School, and Edna's husband, Bert, worked for 28 years at the Birmingham Mint. Sadly he died aged just 43. He was a brass caster and was loved by everyone he met.*

Iris M. Britton went to Camden Street Senior girls in 1945 along with Gladys Morgan. She remembers that the family's fish and chip shop was a few doors down from the 'Gate' pub, and in later years all around the shop were large photos of Gladys, who by then had become Birmingham's Miss Beauty Queen. She had also become an actress, changing her name to Lisa Daniels: 'Her mom would love you to ask about Gladys, who by this time had gone to America and was doing very well making several films. One old film was recently on TV with Bette Davis and Joan Collins, and Lisa had a small part as Bette Davis's hand maiden.' Iris still has both the programme of a school play in which Gladys took part, and a photo of her school pal after she became an actress. She recalls Gladys 'as a lovely girl, never conceited, who would always smile and say hello when she was at home'.

Warstone Lane. This is where the road stopped, although from there to the bottom of Hockley Hill ran a track with no name. Apart from the brewery, there was only one other building on Icknield Street and that was the 'Navigation School'. Still, Brum was approaching fast and, by the 1820s, Camden Street had been cut out of the slopes leading up from Icknield Street. Within a decade, Pope Street and Carver Street were also obvious and Icknield Street now ran all the way to Hockley Hill. In the process, it had become the westernmost boundary of the built-up area of Brum.

Interestingly, some maps indicate that Icknield Street was but a continuation of Wharstone Lane (now Warstone Lane). However, by the late 1830s it had appeared as a road in its own right and perhaps the adoption of the name of the ancient roadway was encouraged by the presence of Icknield House nearby in Monument Lane. This was the home of Timothy Smith, a leading figure in Birmingham's affairs and a prominent member of the committee which pushed for a rail link with London.

By the late 1800s, Icknield Street had been transformed from a rural lane on the outskirts of Brum into one of the city's most important routes, connecting the road to Smethwick and Dudley with that to Handsworth and West Bromwich. Long and fairly wide, it brought together Brookfields and Hockley and was dominated by the bridge of Hockley Station and by three major buildings: Icknield Street School, opened in 1883; the Birmingham Mint – on the site of Forest's Brewery; and Bulpitt's on the corner with Summer Hill. Bulpitt's has now gone – along with so many of the shops which once thrived on Icknield Street – and the school has closed. But thankfully, through its coins, the Mint continues to send Brum's name around the world. It's funny isn't it? The Romans were also famous for their coins.

Still A Village: Marston Green

He was a man whose trade struck deep into time out of memory. For hundreds upon hundreds of years, men like Fred Stanton of Marston Green had been vital figures in any community, swinging their hammers and beating into shape white hot iron. And like the untold numbers of fashioners of metal who had gone before him, Fred was a man whose craft bonded him and his forge with the elements. Just to stand at the entrance to his smithy set the mind and spirit racing to the powerful natural forces which once had ruled the lives of men and women. The raw iron itself had been hewn from the earth – as had those lumps of coal which could be enraged by the air thrust upon them by the working of the bellows. Then there was the redness of the fire itself

FREE HOUSE.
NSELL'S
LES Propr
R. COLES

83-5.   Ye Olde Bell Inn, Marston Green.

The 'Old Bell Inn' at Marston Green in the early years of the twentieth century. Thanks to Roy White. By the 1930s, next to the pub stood Moseley's sweet factory, where Margaret Prichard's dad was the caretaker. The family lived in an army hut at the side of the main building and although there were few amenities, I loved having a bath in a big molasses barrel from the factory. They also had one of the first automatic wrapping machines and there were huge concrete mixer-type things that coated raisins and nuts with chocolate, toffee boilers and large beds of jelly ready for cutting up. In the glass ceiling were thousands of wasps but the toffee men never seemed to get stung.' At the back of the factory was a big lawn and lovely rose gardens, and to the rear of them were workers' allotments. Margaret also remembers that she and her dad used to collect mushrooms from the cricket field behind the 'Bell'.

which blew from it gleeds which gleamed as if they were bobowlers caught in the glow sent out by a candle or a lamp. And, of course, the blacksmith had always close at hand, a bucket of water into which he lunged now and then so as to dowt the hot light of the metal.

Yet, for all that his skills took him so far into the past, now they were brought to bear upon the needs of the modern world – and in that wise so they heralded the coming to an end of the life known by Fred Stanton and his fellow villagers. For in that autumn of 1934, as much as Fred shoed horses, so did he sharpen the picks of the blokes who were building the first of the new houses which were set to transform Marston Green into a suburb of Birmingham. Not that the countryside was banished from the district in one fell swoop. For much of the 1930s, it was large detached houses which were constructed locally and most of the farms carried on as they had done for centuries.

Amongst them was Chapel House Farm, straddling the parishes of Sheldon and Bickenhill – to the latter of which belonged Marston Green. The farm boasted 'sound, well-watered pasture and fertile arable land' and as well as the raising of cattle and the cultivation of corn, its tenant kept ducks and pigs and had an orchard. The farm itself had been owned until 1919 by the Digbys of Coleshill – a family which had gained

Children at Marston Green School, 1921. The teacher on the far left of the back row is Miss Tart, whilst Doll Bloxham stands in front of her on the second row and two along from her is Marge Barber. This and the photo of Chapelfield Farm are in Margaret Francis, Marston Green, Down Memory Lane *(Merstone Publications: 1999).*

Chapelhouse Farm was probably the site of the original chapel of Saint Leonard which was dedicated in 1549. It was owned for many years by the Wingfield Digby Estate which sold the farm and many others locally in 1919. Twenty years later, the site of the farm and its surroundings became Marston Green Golf Course, and the farmhouse was finally demolished in 1981 to make way for the runway extension at Birmingham Airport.

Norah Clift's family moved to the farm in 1931 from the Glebe Farm at Yardley which was taken over by Birmingham Corporation so as to build council houses. She and her three sisters were still at school. In those days 'Marston Green was a delightful place to live. It had a very active social club and dramatic society at the village hall and I remember my younger sister taking part in "Charlie's Aunt". There were dances and various other amusements in the hall and also a keep fit class.' The village also boasted hockey and cricket teams and 'we played matches with Betty and Tommy Wyatt, the sister and brother of Bob Wyatt, the England and Warwickshire captain, at Meriden on the archery ground'.

The farm itself was part of the Maxstoke Priory and there was a stew pond there: 'As children we had a wonderful time boating on it and a difficult time every day trying to round up the ducks which had to be penned in at night because of foxes. Unfortunately there was a public footpath through our rickyard and one night a courting couple must have dropped a cigarette. The signal man at the level crossing tried to alert us by ringing his bell, but couldn't, of course, leave his box to contact us. My mother and father were woken up by the fierce blaze which lit up their bedroom. My aunt dashed to the farm cottage for the cowman. It was a terrible blaze and the local Birmingham fire brigades spent several days extinguishing it. A crowd of onlookers came from the Coventry Road in the small hours of the morning and thought it was great fun, but it was not, I am afraid, for the farmers. It was a disaster.' Regretfully the Clifts had to leave Chapelhouse Farm in 1939 when it was decided to build an airfield and Mr Clift took over the tenancy of Cofton Hall in Barnt Green.

wide lands in the Forest of Arden as far back as 1495 and which later came to own much of Small Heath. Elsewhere in Marston Green, the Digbys had also owned two small-holdings and a couple of other farms, the first of which was that of Marston Culey – a name which called out to the earliest documentary references to the village. Noted as Merstone in the Domesday Book of 1086, in Old English the word meant the farmstead in or by the marsh. Later, the district was split into two manors, one of which was owned by the de Culys in the 1200s and seems to have been centred on a village which became known as Marston Green.

The other main agricultural property was Elmdon and Newlands Farm. At 254 acres this was the largest farm in Marston Green and later disappeared for the development of Birmingham Airport. Opened in 1939, this new facility was the harbinger of the new order and cut off the village from Bickenhill. Urbanisation gathered pace following the Second World War and was accompanied by the expansion of the airport, thus dooming Marston Hall Farm. The site of the second local manor, that of Marston Wavers, it had been held by the Wavers from the early thirteenth century to the late fifteenth century. Built in the early 1600s, Marston Hall itself was demolished in the early 1980s for the erection of the new airport terminal.

Yet if Marston Green is now firmly attached to the West Midlands conurbation, it still looks to the field of Warwickshire and a few buildings remain which blacksmith Fred Stanton and his fellow villagers would recognise. There's the cottage which was the old bakery and general stores in Land Lane, a pair of Elizabethan cottages now united as one building which overlooks the Garden of Memory, and Ash Tree Cottage which was the original 'Tavern' on the corner of Station Road and Coleshill Road. And for all its expansion, Marston Green clings to the feel of a village.

Coaching Inns and Great Stones: Northfield

It wasn't an easy route, leaving Brum by coach in the 1770s and heading south west to Bristol. The first four miles weren't too bad, but once you'd passed the hamlet of Selly Oak and started to go up Griffin's Hill then the road really got ropey. It was narrow, dirty and pitted with pot holes which made the carriage jolt and jar and shifted you backwards and forwards, almost shoving you out of your seat. The discomfort was made worse by the lines of wagons and pack horses which went along the same way carrying salt from Droitwich as well as iron and coal from the Black Country.

In the summer, this industrial traffic flicked stones hither and thither, cutting up the road for other travellers; whilst in the winter they churned the dirt into a mushy mess so that often the carriage wheels of the stage coaches were swamped and made motionless. No wonder the drivers were chuffed when they'd safely crossed both the Griffin's Brook and Wood Brook and reached the top of White Hill without any hold ups, for at least they'd soon be resting at one of the great coaching houses of the West Midlands – the 'Bell Inn' of Northfield.

Situated about half way between the noted 'Hen and Chickens' of Birmingham and the 'Rose and Crown' at the Lickeys, the 'Bell' was a fine-looking, squarish-type structure which boasted an elegant Queen Anne staircase. It became a house when the Bristol Road was straightened to its present line and a new 'Bell' inn was built alongside it. Owned by Samuel Summers, these premises became the focus of the upper village of Northfield which straggled towards Frankley Beeches Road (then Cock Lane). Until the later 1800s, the settlement consisted of little more than a few

The 'Bell Inn', Northfield, at the turn of the century. Notice the contrast between the horse and carts outside the pub and the open-topped motorised omnibus on the Bristol Road. Thanks to Elsie Fox.

houses, a handful of shop keepers including a pork butcher who killed the local pigs, a blacksmith's, a wheelwright's, a toll house and a brickfield.

On the slopes below the 'Bell' lay the old village with its nailer's cottages huddled about the parish church of St Laurence. Dating back to Norman times – and perhaps with traces of Anglo-Saxon work – the place of worship was well known for its barrel organ which played just three tunes and the inscriptions on its bells which were hung in 1730. They record that 'against our casting some did strive, but when a day for meeting they did fix there appeared but nine against 26'. Besides the church stands the 'Great Stone Inn', named after the ice-age deposit which dominated the corner of the building. Because it later filled the pavement and forced folk into the road, in December 1954 the stone was placed inside the adjoining village pound – where stray animals were kept until their owners paid a fee to reclaim them. Little wonder that the owners of the pub always proclaimed that customers could buy their beer 'by the stone and by the pound.'

The two villages of Northfield were surrounded by farms, many of which were reached only through windy, mysterious, hollow ways cut deep into the land and overhung and enshadowed by gnarled trees. Just as intriguing and enchanting as these

In 1954 the Public Works Department of Birmingham City Council decided to move the great stone in Northfield because it was regarded as a serious menace to road safety. Local residents were angered by the proposal and opposed it. This shot shows youngsters from Saint Laurence's Church School on their way to their extension clasrooms in the church hall. They have stopped at the stone, as they have been taught, and are looking round the corner for oncoming traffic. They would wait there until their teacher came from the back of the crocodile of children to tell them it was safe to move on. Thanks to the Birmingham Evening Mail.

lanes were Bog Wood and Bromwich Wood, Cutler's Rough and Woodcock Hill, Pidgeon House and Weoley Castle and farms such as Bangham Pits, Broadhidley, Genner's, Masonley's, Frogmill and Lyeclose. With places such as these and with its fishponds, springs, old clay pits and corn mills, Northfield was as rural a spot as could be found in the Midlands. Its bond with Old England was made even stronger by the ghost stories linked to Tinker's Farm and the rectory and by its characters such as 'Skinner' Wood, 'Snatch' Hemus and 'Male' Hobbis. A strong woman was Hobbis and with her white horse and cart, she was responsible for bringing the washing of the wealthy of Edgbaston to and from the women of the twin villages.

With the Greater Birmingham Act of 1911, Northfield became a district of its bigger neighbour and ceased to be part of Worcestershire. Inexorably its farms disappeared: Tessal Farm house became a garage; Yew Tree Farm was transformed into a housing estate; Hogg's Farm was sunk beneath Frankley Reservoir; and on Lower Shenley Farm emerged shops, flats and Green Meadow Primary School. Amongst the last fields to go were those of Street, Scotland, Ley Hill, Lucas and Hole Farms. This latter was next to 'The Davids', the home of Laurence Cadbury, and was run by Miss 'Dolly' Garland who supplied many of the new folk of Northfield with milk, fruit and vegetables, fruit, eggs, bedding plants and vegetables.

Standing on the Bristol Road now, it's hard to look at the past, but stroll down nearby Bell Holloway and ancient Northfield still speaks.

Gladys Owen, née Faultless, came to live in Northfield when she was seven in the early 1930s. There were no buses on the estate and no local school and so for her schooling she had to walk along the Bristol Road, past the 'Traveller's Rest' to the Masonic Hall. Then Trescott Road School was built and this photo which she sent in shows Gladys in her first year there. She is third from the right in the second row from the front. Gladys was married in Saint Laurence's Church, Northfield and her bridesmaid was Ethel Powell, the girl in the white dress in the front row. There were 46 children in the class and the teacher's name was Miss Peace, whilst Mr Blundell was the headmaster.

From Hamlet to Council Estate: Yardley Wood

It was one of those things that always puzzled you as a kid. Why was it that Yardley Wood was so far away from Yardley? What was the connection between the two places? And then one day it became obvious when you learned that for hundreds of years, Yardley had been separate from Birmingham. In fact, it hadn't joined the city until 1911, having been first a manor and then a town in Worcestershire. And the old Yardley had been much greater than its modern area, for it had stretched narrow and long up the River Cole from Stechford, through Hay Mills, Greet, Tyseley, Sparkhill, Springfield, Acocks Green and Hall Green to Yardley Wood. So there it was. Yardley Wood once had been the wooded part of the ancient parish of Yardley.

Harry Hodges moved to Yardley Wood in April 1926 when he was five. There was no road, only the cut out base where it was going to be and this had big boulders in the bottom ready to take the chipppings and then the tar. It was all wonderful 'out in the country after coming from Stour Street in Ladywood'. Harry went to the little school, which is now the Neighbourhood Office, as the big school had not been built. People were moving into the houses so quickly they had not even been built. The Hodges' house was at 79, Cleve Road and after they arrived the plaster was still drying and it had no electricity for two day and no glass in the windows upstairs. This photo sent in by Harry Hodges is of the Yardley Wood Fishing Club and was taken in 1930. Harry's dad formed the club in May 1926 and is sitting on the basket on the left.

Like the nearby Billesley Common and Swanshurst Common, Yardley Wood was a grazing area open to everyone locally until 1847, after which it was enclosed in fields. That move led to two main farms: the wonderfully-named Quagmire Farm, close to the modern Pendeen Road; and Titterford Farm by Titterford Mill. In the twentieth century, the council changed Titterford to Trittiford as it was felt that the former name might be embarrassing. Two years after the enclosure of Yardley Wood, Miss Sarah Taylor of Moor Green, Moseley paid for the building and the endowment of a church locally. The Taylors were major landowners in this part of Birmingham, having gained their wealth through the manufacturing endeavours of John Taylor. Acclaimed as the Brummagem button king, he and his son had also joined forces with the Lloyds to form Taylor and Lloyd's Bank.

The new place of worship was called Christ Church and it was well needed, for if the local farming folk wished to attend Sunday services they had to traipse a long way to Saint Mary, Moseley, the Church of the Ascension in Hall Green or Saint Nicolas in King's Norton. Probably because of the smallness of the population hereabouts, Christ Church itself became the centre of a large parish which included parts of not only of Yardley but also of King's Norton. In later years, the parish shrank in size with the opening of Saint Agnes, Wake Green, Holy Cross, Billesley and Immanuel, Highter's Heath.

Even before Christ Church had been consecrated there had been a school for Anglican children in Yardley Wood. It had opened in 1838 in School Road, in a building which was also used for public worship. This school was closed in the mid-1880s, although it re-opened in 1889. A year later it was transferred to the Yardley School Board and in 1893 a new school was built in the aptly-named School Road. Like all such places, it later came under the control of Birmingham's education department.

Despite the presence of the long-established school and the beautiful church, no village or even hamlet grew up in Yardley Wood. As late as 1914, there were just a few houses throughout the district and most were to be found on Priory Road, between Scriber's Lane and Slade Lane. Prominent amongst the buildings here were the 'Dog and Partridge' public house and a Baptist Chapel. This last structure had been erected in 1888 as a village station for the great chapel in Cannon Street and had emerged from prayer meetings held in a local cottage. The Slade Lane Chapel was replaced in 1935 by a new place of worship on the Yardley Wood Road.

In the twenty years after the end of the First World War, more changes swept over Yardley Wood than had done so in the previous thousand years. The face of the district was transformed rapidly as hundreds of council houses were erected as part of the laying out of the Billesley Estates. Yardley Wood itself was a clearly defined district within this development. It was bounded to the north by the Chinn Brook; to the east by the River Cole; to the west by the Yardley Wood Road; and to the south by open land, beyond which was Solihull. By 1939, roads had filled in the space between Glastonbury Road and Riversdale Road and after the Second World War, the corporation built another but smaller estate across Priory Road and off Slade Lane –

whilst private houses were constructed around Bach Mill Drive. Yet if the farms of Yardley Wood have gone then still you can feel, smell and imagine the past as you roam around the Tritterford Pool and wander along the cut.

The Coronation Day Street Party in Moorside Road, Yardley Wood, 1953. As you can see by the clothing, it was a cold day. Thanks to Margaret Holloway, née Goode, who was christened at Yardley Wood Church by the vicar, Reverend Isa Rees Jones. Born in March 1930, Margaret recalls that the old vicarage was 'a big house, full of very dark, highly polished furniture. In the hall was a huge chair almost like a throne, carved and very highly polished. A nose of a sword fish was hung on the wall. We whispered when we visited. We were not frightened but very subdued. The vicar's wife used to hold lovely garden parties and the garden itself was long and narrow with lots of roses everywhere.' Yardley Wood Social Club also played a large part in Margaret's childhood as her father was one of the founder members. There were other buildings of note, like the windmill on Priory Road. Local moms and dads used to tell the children that the miller made his journey with his sack of sleep, came past each bedroom, scattered it and returned home. Also on this photo are family members of S. Pegg and Sue MacBeath's mother, aunt, grandmother and neighbour, 'with whom I lived for a short time as a child, her daughter and son, who later went on to run a Lapworth village stores and their baby'. Mrs A. Nickolson is another person pictured, in her case with her two daughters, then aged nine and five. She remembers that she 'was trying to get my younger daughter to join in the children's fancy dress competition. I'd made her a Queen of Hearts dress with crepe paper, but she was determined not to get dressed up for any party. I remember chasing her up the back garden to get her to wear the dress but she had got other ideas.' Mrs Nickolson is towards the back of the group on the left-hand side and is in the dark coat, holding her hair down from the wind.

Vera Rutherford, née Myring, went to Yardley Wood Junior School at first and then was transferred to Our Lady of Lourdes Roman Catholic Junior School, where she joined the choir. This snap of hers shows her fourth from the left in the back row. Father Murphy is in the front row and standing on the left is Mr Powell, the organist for the choir. The photo itself was taken after Vera had left Our Lady of Lourdes and gone to grammar school, 'but a few of us "oldies" remained in the choir'. Vera mentions that also in the group are Sheila and Ann Shortt, Kathleen Butler, Jean Mayhew and Veronica Latham. Vera lived in Priory Road and at the bottom of their long garden was Trittiford Park. In really bad winters the local kids played and skated on the park pond which was frozen over.

Chapter 3:

Hard Collar

Mark of Quality: The Assay Office

There could never have been a Birmingham without men and women who had a vision of what might be. Men like Peter de Bermingham, the lord of the manor in the 1160s, who believed that he could turn Birmingham from an insignificant agricultural hamlet into a major market centre. Men like Joseph Chamberlain, mayor from 1873-6, who dreamed of transforming Birmingham from a place derided for its unambitious council into a place praised as the best governed city in the world. And women like Louisa Ann Ryland who felt that she could change the overcrowded Brum of the nineteenth century into a place noted for its parks which were laid out for the use of everyone.

Matthew Boulton was another visionary. One of the greatest and most gifted figures in the history of Birmingham, his talents were many and his effects on our city were long-standing. The son of a local manufacturer, he began to make his mark nationally and internationally after he opened the Soho Works in Handsworth in 1762. This Temple of the Vulcanian Arts was the largest manufactory in the world and from it, Boulton's workers sent out a host well-crafted and attractive articles like buckles, buttons, toys – small metal goods – ornate pieces made in Sheffield Plate, and ormolu – objects fashioned in gilded bronze.

Boulton and his Soho Works had a fine reputation, but still he was faced with two problems. First, the word Brummagem was the most common name for Birmingham and unfortunately it was seen as a negative one by outsiders. Even now, the Oxford English dictionary defines Brummagem as meaning base or counterfeit were. This bad name had been gained because some of Birmingham's smiths were prone to make false coins. The second problem preoccupying Boulton was that by law, silver items had to be assayed – tested to determine their ingredients and quality. The nearest assay office to Birmingham was 72 miles away at Chester. Obviously, it was costly to send goods that far and it was also possible that they might be damaged or stolen and that their designs might be copied. Boulton was resolved to overcome these difficulties and in 1771 he declared to Lord Selburne that 'I am very desirous of becoming a great silversmith, yet I am determined never to take up that branch in the Large Way I intended unless powers be obtained to have a Marking Hall in Birmingham'.

Not only would such an assay office substantially lower Boulton's costs but also it would enhance Birmingham's reputation, for then the town would be seen as a place which was keen to ensure that its wares were of the highest quality. Boulton sought advice from his friend the Earl of Dartmouth of Sandwell Park, West Bromwich and it was decided to promote an act of Parliament for the establishment of a Birmingham Assay Office. Carefully gaining the backing of other local manufacturers, his customers and influential members of the gentry, Boulton built up a groundswell of support. His hand was strengthened when the Sheffield Cutler's Company asked if he would 'take the workers in plate at Sheffield into the scheme, so as to go hand to hand with you to Parliament and to be comprehended in the same act'.

Fred Jones is in the forefront of this picture. Thanks to the Birmingham Evening Mail. Fred started work at the Assay Office in 1906. He was a silver chain marker, earning 16 shillings for 50 hours work. In those days 'we used to get through a lot of work – up to sixty dozen silver chains a day. Jewellers used to bring us work in the mornings, and delivery boys would return it in a horse and cart in the afternoons. They used to wear a dark blue uniform with shiny buttons and a peaked cap, and they had a half an hour each morning to clean their uniforms and shine their buttons.' Later Fred became a gold hallmarker and then an assayer and he ended his career as foreman of the scraping department. He retired in September 1973, when this photograph was taken. Fred was 84 and would have stayed on longer at work, except that the journey from his home in South Yardley was getting too much for him.

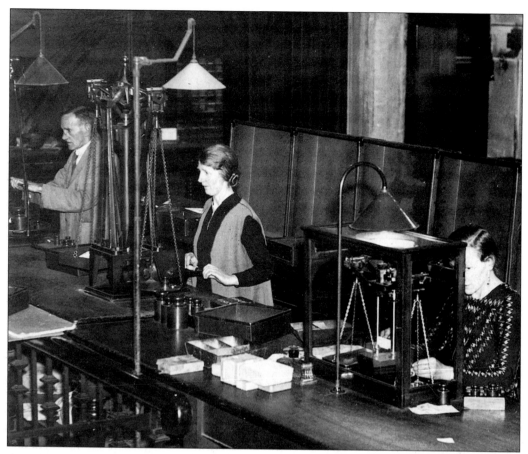

Assay Office workers weighing the articles to ensure that the weight given by the makers agrees with that found by the Assay Office, 1946. Thanks to the Birmingham Evening Mail. Roy D. Smith started work at the Assay Office in 1961 and 'was immediately aware of the wonderful building. It was like stepping back in time 200 years. My first job was laboratory assistant and refinery assistant and I worked with an old man, well past retirement date, called Charlie Tanner. He was very kind to me and a real character who told me many stories of his youth and experiences.' Indeed, many of the people who worked at the Assay Office were very old and were characters. Among them was Tom Pass. He used to crack old-fashioned jokes all the time and 'laugh his socks off' after telling them" He also used to talk of his time abroad in the Boer War and the First World War. Some of the other old-timers included Harry Butler and Frank Little.

In the refinery, Roy worked with Les Rutledge and the foreman was David Eames. This section was 'just like an alchemist's den and I spent many happy hours in there'. In those days, the workers were allowed to play table tennis during the dinner hour, or else they could have a drink at the bar, adjacent to the refinery, and which was run by Tubby Dawes. Once a year, a dividend was paid out to those folk who had spent money over the bar – the amount depending upon the particular sum and the bar's profits. Roy still fondly recalls many of his workmates such as Irish Maggie, Geoff Savage, Les Haynes and 'the wonderful Beatrice Hickman who gave me a lot of good advice and help. She was a delightful lady.' Roy has no doubt that 'I spent some of the best times of my working life in the Assay Office and I would love to go there again'. One of Roy's memorable jobs was the hallmarking of medals to commemorate the landing of men on the moon.

Still, Boulton's plans were attacked by the silversmiths and goldsmiths of London. They 'were up in arms' about the possibility of Birmingham gaining its own assay office, but Boulton and his allies had a clear answer to them: 'it is surprising that any opposition should be made to granting this town an Assay-Master, which produces more Manufacturers in Gold and Silver than all the other towns put together, and is universally acknowledged the Seat of Manufacturing Ingenuity in the kingdom'. Such an argument could not be gainsaid and with vigour and tenacity Boulton pressed Birmingham's case. He was rewarded on May 28, 1773 when the necessary act was given the Royal Assent. Boulton had been in the capital for the occasion and when he returned in triumph to Birmingham he was greeted with the peeling of the local church bells.

Three months later, the Birmingham Assay Office opened when it leased three rooms at the 'King's Head Inn', New Street. With its mark of an anchor, the Assay Office rapidly established itself as a major facility within Birmingham and its existence was responsible for an upsurge in the trade of silversmiths and goldsmiths in the town. Since 1877, the Assay Office has been at its impressive offices in Newhall Street, opposite the old Science Museum. Now as then, it continues to test and mark the silver and gold wrought in Birmingham and now as then, it is a vital feature in pushing forward the reputation of our city.

Princess Margaret visted the Assay Office on May 2, 1951 and here she is shown how to mark a gold badge for the Lord Mayor of Birmingham and silver table lighter for the Lord Mayor's Parlour. The man helping her to press on the Assay Office's symbol of an anchor is Tom Bedford, the gold hallmarking foreman. Overlooking Tom, the tall man is Mr Hamil Westwood, then Deputy Assay Master to his 85 year old father and the fourth person in his family to hold that post. Hamil Westwood later took over from his father. To his right are three wardens of the Assay Office and then Mr Boultbee Brooks, the senior warden. Another warden stands beside Mr Brooks and the man with chain of office is the Lord Mayor of Birmingham, Alderman A. Paddon Smith.

This photograph was sent to me by Eve Bilson, née McGlacken, who began work at the Assay Office as an office junior on January 1, 1950 – in the days when New Year's Day was not a holiday. She worked there for ten years, gaining a lot of experience in accounts and secretarial work. On the retirement of the Assay Master's secretary she was promoted to become secretary to Mr Hamil Westwood, a position Eve held until 1960 when she left to start a family. Her time at the Assay Office was very happy and she especially recalls the Boulton Room as a special place because of its wonderful collection of silver which was the pride and joy of the wardens.

One of the other workers who met Princess Margaret was the Tom Pass mentioned by Roy D. Smith. His daughter, Mrs Elsie Sumner, states that apart from four years army service in The First World War, her father spent all his working life at the Assay Office. He was one of the hallmarkers who tested and marked the items of gold and wore a black apron 'which was never washed but was put in the "Muffer" (furnace) in order to recover the minute deposits of gold'. When Thomas completed his first 25 years service, he was presented with a Britannia silver medal, which unfortunately was stolen in a robbery at home. A member of the Assay Office Air Rifle Club, Thomas retired when he was in his mid 70s. He was still riding his bicycle to work up to that point.

Poles, Shaves and Haircuts: Barbers

Looking back to his childhood days, it seemed that not only did every kind of shop have its own peculiar feel but also it had its own special fascination. There was the chemist's raising up visions of tales of the 'Arabian Nights' with its alluring glass bottles each filled with water coloured as mauve, green or deep red. There was the grocer's shop with that enigmatic door behind the counter, through which the assistant would disappear to fetch goods from who knows where. And there was the outdoor, which hinted at the hidden world of grown ups behind the empty bottles of beer which stood between the window and the net which veiled off the goings on inside.

Then there was the barber's shop. It had an almost enchanting effect upon him. He'd stand outside it for ages, just looking at the red and white stripes painted spirally on a pole which hung from the front wall. Sometimes the pole appeared as if it were a great stick of rock which was waiting to be licked. On other occasions it looked as if its scrolling stripes were alive and moving and were drawing him spellbound into another world. And now and then his dreams shifted to the pole becoming the symbol of his bravery, as he was held up to it by his pals so that he could hang up his country's flag in defiance of the powerful enemy. Many's the time he'd asked his dad about the significance of the pole, even though he knew the answer before it was told him – that in days gone by when people couldn't read, each retailer was marked out by a sign so as to catch the eye of shoppers. The only other place that was made so distinctive nowadays was the pawnshop and its three brass balls repelled him, shouting out to him

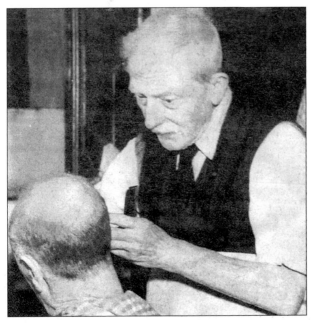

Thomas Adderley is cutting the hair of his son-in-law. According to his grand-daughter, Mrs A. Shemmans, Thomas was the oldest barber in Birmingham when he retired aged 82. He came to his shop at 4, Sampson Road, Camp Hill when he was sixteen years of age and seven years later he married his wife at Saint Alban's Church, Highgate. Thomas died in 1954 in his ninetieth year and was a well known figure and in his early years he used to go to the prisons and shave the men. His grand-daughter has some wonderful memories of him as she was born nearby in Sandy Lane and was always with her grandparents. When she was young, she and the other youngsters in the family all did their share to help and Mrs Shemmans used to take Thomas's scissors to be sharpened in Pershore Street. In those days it was 4d for a shave and 6d for a haircut. Thanks to Mrs Shemmans and Val Whitehouse.

The premises of Farmer the Palmer at 156, Icknield Port Road, about 1911. Thanks to Carl Thomas.
Rose Cooper's dad, Edward Barber, had a shop such as this one at 1 Berkley Street, to which he'd
moved from nearby Broad Street in about 1912. It had a bay window on the roof of which was a
window box filled with gladiolas. Behind the window lay the shop, at the rear of which was the
family's kitchen. The charge for a shave was 2d and for a haircut it was 4d. There were shelves of
shaving pots, 'all with gold numbers on. My way of learning the six times table. If there were more
than six customers waiting they would go away and come back. One customer I remember was hard
up and had his shave first and then couldn't pay so he went home, painted flowers on glass and
made two pictures to pay for it.' Edward's red and white pole was washed down every week.

Eric Workman left school in 1938 and became a lather boy in the barbers in his own street,
Cattell Road. In the first years, he just lathered up for more experienced barbers to shave and
watched how the hairs were cut. During that time it was all 'short back and sides', apart from a few
customers who had a 'regency', a slightly longer cut with a bit more shape. After his war-time
service, Eric resumed his trade as a barber on the Soho Road and then took over the shop in Cattell
Road. In the 1950s, he cut the hair of many of the Blues players and today, based at the Grange
salon on the Cov, he cuts the hairs of King Pleasure and the Biscuit Boys. He can claim over 50
years of barbering and to the folk of Small Heath he is simply, Eric the Barber.

as they did of his mom's weekly visit with her bundle of washing and the hard times they were having to live through.

But it wasn't just the pole that attracted him to the barber's. There was so much else about the shop that was engrossing. Like the fact that it belonged exclusively to men and that when you went in, there was yapping and banter and you could imagine yourself as part of the grown-up world of blokes. How desperately you wished you understood the double meanings, the raised eyebrows, the shifts of the head, the outward palming of the hands, the deep breaths and the short snorts! How keenly you wished that you too could make the telling remark that would cut someone down to size, or crack the sharp one liner that would have everyone guffawing, or pass on the vital piece of information that each person prized so much and which led to approving mutters of 'He knows 'is stuff, y'know'.

There was so much that was interesting about the barber's shop, like the secrecy with which the regulars would palm over a bet to the man shaving them or cutting their hair. Everyone knew that some barbers doubled up as illegal bookies and that their proper trade acted as a blind to the coppers who found it so hard to catch out their suspect. But of course, much of the glamour of the shop was down to the barber himself. It was funny how so many shopkeepers took on the look of their business. Like butchers always seemed to be large and ruddy, whilst barbers always appeared as thin and upright as the poles which hung outside their shops.

Perhaps the thing above all that grabbed his eyes was the way in which the barber was able to chat to a customer whilst doing his job. It was amazing how he'd be canting away as his left index finger would lift up the punter's chin so that his right hand could sweep below and fell the bristles with the cut throat razor. What skill there was in shaving and how much trust the vulnerable customer had in the barber's ability not to cause injury. Rarely was someone's skin nicked and blood caused to flow. How swiftly and carefully the barber worked, and how dexterously did he sharpen up his razor on the strop which hung from a hook on the wall. There was no doubt about it. Barbers did have a craft and how ever they learned it was as mysterious as the shops that they ran.

Taken in the 1950s, this gent's hairdressers was on the corner of Talford Street and Upper Webster Street, Aston. Thanks to Johnny Landon. Between 1953 and 1961, the shop was run by John Mobley who lived above the shop with his wife, Beryl. Both are pictured on this shot. John is the taller of the two men standing by the car on the left, whilst Beryl is the lady with the broom. The posters on the wall to the right of the shop were compulsory purchase notices indicating that the premises were to be knocked down. Despite this, the landlord later rebuilt the front of the shop and the house.

The shop on the other corner, 55, Webster Street, had been owned by Mrs Sarah Brotherhood, who also had the adjoining premises at 53, Webster Street, where she used to take in artistes from the Aston Hippodrome, giving them bed and breakfast. In 1945, it was bought by the mother of Molly Williams, née Hinton, and her partner. They moved there from Droitwich when Molly was twelve, and her mother was helped in running the shop by her older daughter. In fact it was known as Betty's shop after this sister, although the name above the door was W. Boucher. The women built up a lovely selection of jars of sweets which were always displayed in the window and 'we also sold cigarettes, bread, milk and potatoes. The children's favourite was ice lollies, all different colours for 1d each.'

Behind the shop was a large blue, sliding gate into a coalyard: 'we had about 12 barrows and when the coal delivery arrived (as that was also on ration), the customers would see it come and be down to try and get theirs. So many a dinner time from Burlington Street School I spent helping to weigh cwts of coal into barrows which emptied quicker than we could fill them.' The shop itself was open from eight in the morning till eight at night Monday to Saturday and from nine in the morning till twelve noon on Sundays. There were some lovely customers, one of whom was a lady who had never seen the sea: 'so it was decided a customers' outing was called for. They each paid a little a week until there was enough in the kitty to hire a char-a-banc and off we all went to New Brighton. It was such a success that it was followed by a few mystery trips in the evenings in and around Bewdley and Evesham.' The family sold the shop in 1952 and it was then run by Mrs Margaret Wilson.

Hard Water and Good Beer: Dares Brewery

It was the well packed sandstones beneath the ground which coloured Brummagem a burned red. Known properly as Keuper Sandstone, it was dug out and baked to provide the bricks which built the town. It had another major impact, too. For the sandstone yielded supplies of water which were plentiful, easily-reached and essential to the development of Birmingham. Throughout the city, wells were sunk to provide water both for drinking and industrial purposes. There were great public wells like that in Digbeth, which gave its name to Well Street, but one of the most noted of all the wells was that belonging to Dares Brewery on Belgrave Road.

For over 100 feet, it struck straight and true into the slope which rose up from the River Rea to the ridge along which runs Moseley Road. The water it gave up was cold,

James William Hussey and his second wife, Phoebe, were caretakers at Dares Brewery until about 1923. This photo was sent in by Audrey Bagby, née Hussey, whose father, James, also worked at Dares for a short time before he went into the army. It shows his half brother, Jack, his half sisters, Edna and Kath and a couple of their friends and was taken outside the brewery.

hard and of an outstanding character. So pure was it, that the company brewed a bitter so clear that you could place a newspaper behind a full pint and still be able to read the affairs of the day. Like so many large-scale breweries, the company had begun in a small way. It was founded by William Dares in the 1870s, when he ran the 'Turks Head' at 16 Highgate Street – just up from The Bend in Gooch Street. But as the 1870s flittered out, Will Dares transformed himself into a brewer of substance by buying the land between his pub and Belgrave Road. Here, halfway between Sherlock Street and Frank Street in Highgate, he built the grand South End Brewery.

Will was happy enough selling his beer to the increasing number of publicans who did not want the bother of brewing their own ale, but under his son, John Henry, the company was led into a new direction – the purchase of tied houses. This move gave Dares a guaranteed outlet for its ales. The brewery's popularity with clubs and independent publicans arose from the powerful attributes of Dares Bitter. It was a popular brew and its superior quality was acclaimed in 1937 at the Brewer's Exhibition. Out of 700 entries from across the world, Dares was voted the best draught

William Andrews, the father of Mrs D. Bristall, was foreman brewer at Dares and the family lived in the caretaker's house next to the brewery for over 25 years. William believed that it was the very hard water from Dares artesian well which made the brewery's beer so good. People often came to the door asking for some of the water as 'they believed it was good for their eyes'. Dares was a family firm and most of the workers had long service with the firm. This photograph sent in by Mrs Bristall shows some of them on a works fishing outing in the 1930s. James Allder was the father of Sylvia Smith and he worked for Dares for about twelve years before he died. He was a driver/drayman and during the Blitz he was hardly ever home before midnight because he used to travel very long distances to army camps and air force bases 'and often had to walk home long distances because of the air raids and bombing'. He was a very keen fisherman and is third from the left on the top row in this photograph.

beer. At the following year's event, the company won another award for its gold medal bottled beer which had been brewed by Peter Dares, one of John Henry's four sons. All the brothers were steeped in the traditions of brewing and all were experts in their field, having gained qualifications in their craft from The University of Birmingham. Sadly,

The 'White Horse' pub, a Dares house, stood on the corner of Macdonald Street, along which the photographer is looking, and Bishop Street. Thanks to Johnny Landon

Val Smith worked as private secretary to the three directors of Dares Brewery for five years from about 1958. She recalls that Wilfred, the senior, was responsible for the brewery side; Neville was the company secretary; and Aubrey worked on the sales side. All three were answerable to 'old man Dares, their father, to whom they reported once a week.' It was a good old-fashioned traditional brewery 'with not many workers, but all of whom had been with the family business for many years'. After the Dares business was sold to Davenport's, Val continued to work for a very short time 'just to assist with the paperwork and showing the new bosses the ropes'.

Bernice Latimer, then Clifford, started at Dares in 1955 when Bill Laight was office manager and when Charles Tranter and Len Knight were on orders and despatch. Others she remembers are Charlie Havercroft on free trade, Margie Lines on accounts, Doreen Beardsmore in charge of managed houses, and Charlie Hope and Mr Meek in the office. Bernice herself was a comptometer operator, working out the stocks that the stocktaker, Ron Latimer, used to take daily to pubs and hotels. The two of them transferred to Davenport's in 1961 and with love blossoming, they married in 1963. Sadly, Ron has passed away, but Doreen has wonderful memories of a happy marriage.

Peter was killed in action in the Second World War, after which his brothers took over. H. 'Bill' Dares was the MD. He was active not only in the business but also in the affairs of Birmingham. For many years, he was a councillor and director of Birmingham City Football Club. One of the other brothers, Aubrey, was responsible for modernising the public houses and for the managers and it was he who came up with the name of Dares Drum Bitter, 'the bitter you can't beat'.

Unfortunately, the brewery itself did not survive as an independent firm. It was taken over by Davenport's and was knocked down as the Inner Ring Road slithered around the city. Today there is nothing left to recall Dares of Highgate. The company is gone and the well is hidden from view. Still, many can recall the taste of one of the finest bitters in the world – Dares.

Building Brum: Elvins

Since 1166 when Brum first got a market and set itself on making its name, there have been only two constants in our history. What are they? Why the Bull Ring, of course, and change. With no natural, physical or geographical reasons to explain our rise to become a major world city, Birmingham has forever had to adapt, innovate and alter. If we had not done so, we would never have thrust ourselves into history and we would have remained an insignificant village. As one of our trades has declined so we have had to shift swiftly to another – and only by so doing have we been able to wrest for ourselves the titles of the Toyshop of Europe, the City of a Thousand Trades and the Workshop of the World.

This speed in finding new items to manufacture has been matched by our swiftness in changing the look of our city. Each generation of Brummies seems to want to sweep away the past and reforge Birmingham in its own image. No sooner have houses,

The 'Broadway' Cinema on the corner of Wrentham Street and Bristol Street was built by Elvins in 1922-23 at a cost of £12,867. Thanks to Bill Askew. This building replaced the 'Bristol Picture House' which had been the 'Electric Picture House'. The film, 'The Stormbreaker' was the first shown at the new 'Broadway' on April 2,1923. After much alteration, the 'Broadway' was renamed the 'Cinephone' in 1956. It specialised then in foreign and X-rated films and was closed down in 1976. As the 'Gala Cinema' and then the 'Climax Cinema', films continued to be shown until 1984.

Workers in the masonry yard of Elvins during the inter-war years. Thanks to Bill Askew. Arthur Kennedy started at Elvins in 1959 as a young bricklayer, after serving his apprenticeship with Percy W. Cox of Grove Lane, Handsworth – 'another old established firm which built the fire station in town and Dame Elizabeth Cadbury's School in Bournville'. Elvins yard and offices were close to the Hockley Palladium and the business was run as very much a family firm, with 'many employees having been with them for years. It was very close knit concern and there were good relationships with the staff.' Arthur points out that Elvins main work was on factory building, alterations and extensions and he himself worked on a number of premises, including one in the Jewellery Quarter and another close to Dudley Road Hospital: 'In those days, you could walk out of one building firm on a Friday and start at another on the Monday. We would never be out of work and it was common for tradesman to chase an extra 6d (2d) an hour at other firms.' The last property Arthur was involved with was the Catholic Church building opposite the 'Country Girl' in Alum Rock. He left Elvins to join the Birmingham City Council Housing Management Department at Bush House in Broad Street.

factories and workshops overlain farmland than those structures themselves have been torn down and another lot put up in their place. Indeed, for so much of our history, Birmingham has been one great building site and in the making of the city itself one vital industry has been overlooked too often – the construction industry.

Just think of some of the great building firms which have been instrumental in creating the Brum that we know. There's Dares with their Distinctive Houses, and whose careful development of Hall Green and other areas in the inter-war years has led to the listing of Miall Road by conservationists. There's Bryant's, a business which was started in the 1880s in Small Heath and which for many years has been a major house builder. Then there are the firms which have focused more on the construction of commercial premises, such as William Sapcote and Sons of Camden Street which started up way back in 1853 and which is still building for Brum. Almost as old were Moffatt and Whittal and T. Elvins and Sons, whose founder fought against powerful odds to make something of himself.

Thomas Elvins was born in 1840 in the Cornish village of Lostwithiel. His dad was a Methodist lay preacher whose principles led him to give up his job in a brewery and to move to help the poor of Birmingham. Affected badly by the polluted atmosphere of the town, George Elvins decided to leave England for the warmth of Australia. He left behind his wife and all his children bar for Thomas. Arriving in the new land, the Elvins went to the gold fields but soon afterwards the father died and Thomas was left alone.

The premises of W. Canning in Great Hampton Street. Thanks to Bill Askew. Elvins began working for Canning's in 1909 when they built new premises in Kenyon Street at a cost of £6,788. A year later they constructed new buildings in Great Hampton Street, but these themselves were replaced with a fresh structure in 1927 for the outlay of £43,866. Elvins continued to be contracted by Canning's into the 1980s.

The months which followed are an amazing story of hardship, single- mindedness and perseverance. Aged just eleven, Thomas earned a few bob as a cook's boy for the miners and then worked his way to the coast where he got himself on a boat as a cabin boy. After a rough passage, he landed at Plymouth – but still his tribulations weren't over for the youngster had to tramp all the way home to his mom in Brum. After some schooling at a Methodist Chapel, Thomas served his apprenticeship as a builder and aged 25 he set up in partnership with a pal. The joint venture didn't last long and after a number of moves, Thomas Elvins and his wife, Sarah, set up business and home at 1 and 3 Naden Road, Handsworth – close to the border with Lozells.

In the succeeding years, Elvins gained a high reputation for his house building but gradually he became involved in large-scale commercial undertakings. His first big contract came in 1895 when Handsworth Urban District Council paid him £226 2s to build a mortuary, and two years later he completed four buildings for the Birmingham District and Counties Bank (later part of Barclays). By the early years of the twentieth century, Elvins and his sons were established as a major force within Birmingham's construction industry and in the succeeding years they carried out the building of many important structures. Amongst them were Digbeth Police Station, Sutton Coldfield Town Hall, The 'Crown' Picture House in Icknield Port Road, the head office of W. Canning's in Great Hampton Street and what is now the accident and emergency department of the Children's Hospital. Although the firm is no longer in operation, such buildings have ensured that the mark of Elvins is clear upon the face of Brum.

Castings and Steel: Gabriel's

It was one of the most famous of Brum's factories. There it stood in Cambridge Street, the works and rolling mills of Robert Walter Winfield, grabbing not only the attention of Brummies but also the keen interest of royalty. For so exquisite was the brassware of Winfield's that it was sought avidly by the wealthy and powerful across the world. At the Great Exhibition of 1851, the company had a prominent position in the 'Birmingham Court' and showed off a gracious gas lamp and bracket which was

Part of the original foundry at Gabriel's. Thanks to Gabriel and Company. W.D. Wilkes got a job at Gabriel's through his cousin who lived just down the road in Doe Street. It was a real family business with Tom Conlon as foreman alongside his brothers George and Sid and his brother-in-law, Jim Webb. Then there were two brothers named Taylor, G. Brown, D. Appleby and Bill Parson who 'kept us happy singing. It was a very close knit firm'. Les Rake left Loxton Street School in 1959 and started straight away at Gabriel's: 'How imposing it felt on that first day. The noise of the overhead belt driven shafts that powered the machinery, the smell of the grease and the subsoil as I followed lamely in the steps of Mr Tom Conlon, the foreman to the shop where I would work. Introduction to the chargehand "Ike" Grice, a feeling of reassurance as he told me not to worry, the lads would look out for me. A glance around the shop as smiles and nods gave me a friendly welcome. After all I was their new errand boy.' Les's first wage was three pounds seven and a tanner. He was rich and is still rich with the memories of characters like Harold Jeavons, 'the everywhere man,' Sammy Ricketts, Kenny Hitchens and Arthur Bluntstone.

bought by Queen Victoria. Amongst the other wonderful works on view were metallic bedsteads, window cornices and curtain bands. Everyone's eyes were drawn to these ornate wares and it seemed that Winfield's would always be at the forefront of manufacturing, not only in Birmingham but also in the western world. Yet for all it fame, Winfield's stumbled after the death of its founder in 1869 and as the twentieth century sprang into history, his firm ceased operations altogether.

This was a sad end for a business started by one of the industrial heroes of Birmingham, but fortunately his descendants have continued to make their mark in the making of things in our city. Although his only son died young, Robert Winfield had two daughters. One of them was Emily and in 1888 she married a Percy Gabriel. A fascinating bloke, Gabriel was the son of the vicar of All Saints, Birmingham and had served his apprenticeship at the renowned Tangye's in Smethwick. Later he became the manager of the National Arms Factory, but in 1884 and aged just 26 he decided to set up on his own. For £235 he bought a small brass foundry concern in AB Row along with its 'pattern, pattern cards, goodwill, plant and stock.' With these and thirteen workers he began Gabriel and Company. Following his marriage, Percy was made a director of R.W. Winfield but the action was too late to be effective and the famous firm passed out of the hands of the family and into a steep decline. Luckily, Percy's own business thrived and in 1896 he purchased the patterns and tools of another small operation and enlarged his factory by leasing the house next door.

True to the tradition of Robert W. Winfield, Gabriel's made eye-catching brass goods, such as drawer handles for cabinet makers and carpenters, and also general brassware, like railings of various kinds. However, by the early years of the twentieth century, the decision had been made to become more specialised and concentrate on making fittings for trams, buses and railway carriages. Soon, Gabriel's boasted a catalogue which included an astonishing range of over 1,700 items and by 1914 the dynamic Percy Gabriel had also developed and patented 'Clarus Metal'. This was a new aluminium alloy which contained copper and chromium. Its great advantage was that it was as light as aluminium itself but was stronger than brass. Clarus Metal proved a success, especially with builders who used it for new bathroom fittings.

That same year there was an extraordinary coincidence which emphasised the importance of Gabriel's products. One night in early September, a lad was riding his bike along Bristol Road when his wheel skidded. The youngster was thrown in front of a passing tram. Swiftly, the driver applied his brakes, whilst the guard on the tram 'acted perfectly and picked up both the lad and his machine'. The eleven-year old boy was harmed only by a slight bruise. He was none other than Edward Gabriel and his life had been saved by the 'Save All' Life Guard which was made by his father's firm.

'Mr Ted' later became managing director of Gabriel's and supervised two major projects. The first was the introduction of stainless steel castings, such as control and brake handles for the City of Birmingham trams; whilst the second was the piecemeal demolition of the old premises of the company and the construction of a new factory. That factory itself has now been knocked down to make way for the exciting

Discovery Centre. Thankfully, Gabriel's has remained in Brum. Determined to stay true to its heritage and close to its skilled workers, the firm is now in Hay Hall Road, Tyseley. Today it has the only foundry in Birmingham which makes sand-moulded steel castings and it continues to make quality products such as hand-rail systems for passenger transport and balustrades for new buildings in the city. Carrying on the traditions of excellence cherished by Robert W. Winfield, Gabriel's and other manufacturers are shouting out that manufacturing does have a major role to play in the Birmingham of the new millennium.

A scene in one of the machine shops at Gabriel's. Thanks to Gabriel and Company. Arthur Evans worked in this shop under Joe Flynn and with his childhood pal, Arthur Murphy. The power and lighting was supplied by two diesel engines 'and one morning when I got to work the water mains had been smashed during the air raids and so another boy and I spent several hours lugging buckets of water from the dairy in Grosvenor Street to fill the cooling tanks'. Tom Broadfield was also in the machine shop at Gabriel's during the war and specialised in central lathe work and made bren gun carrier tow hooks and sea mine detonator horns. The shop was situated on the first floor together with the polishing area and the packing shop, where the girls wrapped up the handrails and other fittings and boxed them ready for despatch. Like other workers, Tom spent a lot of time fire watching on the roof of Gabriel's and 'many nights we stood on the roof watching the centre of town being bombed and on half a dozen occasions watching Curzon Street Railway being bombed. The blasts on these occasions were strong enough to push us back from the edge of the roof where we were watching from.'

Workers at Gabriel's about 1914. Thanks to Gabriel and Company. Edna C. Fell started at Gabriel and Company as a shorthand typist in 1937 and soon became secretary to Mr Edward Gabriel, managing director of the firm. In those days, the offices were in three or four small and very old-fashioned cottages, behind which was the factory which was being rebuilt a small piece at a time. The first thing that struck Edna was the filing system – 'brown paper packets on shelves which covered the whole of one wall of the office and really I thought this was dreadful'. So Edna persuaded Mr Ted to buy a cabinet into which she put all the files. Thereafter, Mr Gabriel christened this fresh method as 'Fell's infallible filing system'.

However, other time-honoured practices of Gabriel's impressed Edna deeply. Everyone in the offices was called by their Christian name, whilst 'at my first Easter with the company, I was amazed when Mr Gabriel sent for each girl in the offices, one at a time, and gave them a little packet with £1 in it. This is what his father had done on every holiday. Well I was amazed, of course I had never heard of this before and I thought it was rather wonderful.' During these years, Gabriel's was doing brass, gun-metal and fairly new stainless steel castings, and as war approached it turned to producing larger castings for the Admiralty. Gabriel's itself was hit by bombing and tragically both of Edna's parents were killed in the air raids.

Bill Fell worked at Gabriel's at the same time. He was maintenance electrician and recalls that there were two sides to the factory, each of which was run by its own Brush twin engines which also generated the electricity for the company. The main foundry was opposite in Duke Street, where Birlec Electric Furnaces were installed during the war and for the upkeep of which Bill was responsible. One old fellow called George Mills lived next to the factory and when the bombings were on he'd shake his fist in the air and shout, 'you couldn't kill me in the last one and you won't in this one'. Unfortunately, George was killed entering Gabriel's just as a bomb hit the building. May he rest in peace.

George Mills was the maternal grandfather of Jean Simmonds and although she was not born till after he died 'his attitude to the air raids was legendary in my family. I was brought up on it. He simply refused to take shelter.' Jean's Mom, Lily, was his youngest child and she adored her dad 'and used to beg him to go down the cellar or in the shelter, but he never did'. When the bomb which killed George exploded, Lily ran back to the house 'and up the stairs, and feeling around in the bed in the blackness to find her father. All she felt were shards of glass, all the windows had been blown in. She knew then where he would be, where he preferred to be, in the thick of it.'

Sauces, Pickles and Chutney: Holbrooks

Although both firms were making vinegar, their merger still seemed a bit strange if only because of the distance between them. On the one hand there was Swan and Company based at the Stourport Pure Malt Vinegar Brewery and in business since 1798. On the other was Tompson, Berry and Tompson of Ashted Row, Birmingham and in operation only since 1860. But if outsiders may have felt that the union was ill-conceived, then insiders realised that it was propelled by the ambitions of one man who was connected to both companies. His name was Edward Collens.

Originally apprenticed to a draper, Collens abandoned this path and moved into the study of chemistry. Regarded as a brilliant student, he married the cousin of James Swan and by the late 1860s was managing the Stourport brewery. Ambitious to get on and bring in improvements, he was thwarted by Swan's lack of interest. Luckily a new opportunity arose. The Birmingham vinegar company of Tompson, Berry and Tompson was struggling. Although Arthur Berry was a maker of British wines, his two partners were maltsters and yet they were faced with problems with their brewing of pure malt vinegar. They realised that they needed the skills of a chemist and so brought in Collens as a partner in 1869.

Holbrooks Factory in Ashted, on the corner of Dartmouth Street and Ashted Row which is running from left to right. Thanks to Pam Evans. The father of Pam Evans, Cecil Alfred Evans, was works manager at Holbrooks and went to Sydney to manage the firm's factory in Australia, returning two years later as he suffered from ill health. His father, Robert Evans, was also at Holbrooks and 'it was always a family story' that he invented Worcestershire sauce.

Eileen Sadler, then Rose, was born in 1920 in Ashted Row at the Holbrooks Sauce and Pickle Works, 'this being the home of an aunt and uncle of my dad, who were resident caretakers there'. In fact, Eileen actually lived at Holbrooks for a time until her parents were able to get a home of their own. Her Granny Rose also worked at the factory in the late 1800s, 'peeling onions for pickling and I believe she was known as the fastest onion peeler in the works'. She reared eleven children in between her job.

Women working in the filling room at Holbrooks. Doris Brittle, née Hateley, came out of Francis Street, just round the corner from Holbrooks, and started at the company in the jelly and custard factory. At first she was an errand girl, taking invoices and messages from one department to another. Doris stresses that it was a lovely place to work in and everyone was very conscientious.

Seven years later the aspiring young chemist secured the amalgamation of the two firms with which he was connected so intimately. Put in charge of both breweries, he swiftly set about introducing new equipment and innovative production techniques. He was supported strongly by John Tompson, who as managing director was adept at choosing the right man for the job. This was made plain by his appointment of Robert Evans, a person who was knowledgeable in the making of sauces and pickles – in which, of course, vinegar was the chief ingredient. Evans was also an able organiser and administrator and it was he who set up a team of representatives to sell the products of what was now J. Tompson Ltd.

It was a successful venture, for backed up by quality products and an efficient service, the reps were selling almost two million bottles and jars of sauces, pickles and chutneys annually by 1879. By this date the company was known as the Birmingham Vinegar Brewery and it was gaining particular attention for one of its sauces. Known as a 'Thin' sauce it was based on a recipe which one worker had brought with him. In turn, this man supposedly had gained expertise in the secret ingredients from 'a nobleman of the county of Worcester' who had been made aware of the sauce during his travels in India.

Although the product was difficult to make, it was becoming very popular and John Tompson recognised the need to market it under a brand name. In 1880 he came up with the title after his chief clerk mentioned that a representative called Holbrook had chosen the sauce for a sales effort and had received great success. In fact, 'Holbrook's sauce orders were amazing'. Within a few years, the name Holbrooks was associated with the whole company and W.D. Holbrook himself went to court to prevent the use of his name in this way. His case failed and in 1893 he emigrated to New Zealand, by which date Holbrooks sauce was selling strongly in Australia and South Africa as well as in Britain.

At home the sauce was associated with a prominent advertising campaign, whereby hoardings were pasted with a strong figure of Shakespeare leaning nonchalantly on orange-labelled bottles of Holbrooks Worcestershire Sauce. The bard's figure was accompanied by an equally eye-catching caption, 'Not for an age but for all time...' Not everything was plain selling, though. Sometimes the sauce continued to ferment after it had left the Ashted factory and on one occasion a bottle popped and the stopper shot into the face of the lady who was purchasing it. This problem was solved by the introduction of pasteurisation.

By the early 1900s, vinegar production was focused on Stourport while all sauces, chutneys and pickles were made at Ashted, where an especially high-grade of water was drawn from artesian wells. Above ground in 'The Farm', a storage yard, were gathered scores upon scores of five hundredweight casks containing fruits and vegetables from across the globe, while the Worcestershire sauce itself was matured in giant wooden vats which collectively held tens of thousands of tons of liquid. These vats were badly damaged in several German air raids at the end of 1940, in one of which sadly a worker called Joseph Brookes was killed while fire watching. Since the early 1950s, Holbrooks has been gone from Ashted – but there are many still who recall its impressive buildings, its distinctive aromas and its wonderful products.

Drivers prepare to set off on their deliveries for Holbrooks. Connie Symonds, then Hastings, tells me that her father worked at Holbrooks for many years. He'd served in the Royal Marines during the Great War and won both the DCM and MM, but when he came out of the forces and married his sweetheart he found that there were no jobs in his trade of organ building and finishing. Fortunately he got a job for a few months at Holbrooks, 'on the understanding that when the carpenter recovered from illness he would leave'. After nine months, he was laid off and he stayed unemployed until Connie was two when Holbrooks took him back on. He stayed with the firm until he was 67 and Connie states that 'his whole life was work'. She and her sister vividly remember taking his dinner to their dad when he was fire watching in the war. They had to go all the way from New Oscott to Dartmouth Street on the tram, 'carrying his dinner in a basin and trying not to spill too much gravy, up Ashted Row where he would wait outside on the further doors for us. Sirens or no sirens we still went. Sometimes he would let us in for there was a snooker table and we loved to watch him and the others playing but it was never for long.'

Bill Taylor was born at 144 Windsor Street right next door to Holbrooks. On the night of November 19 to the morning of the November 20, 1940 the building was firebombed. Bill was in a shelter beneath Holbrooks and like everyone else had to move to another shelter in Ashted Row, emerging to find his home blown up – 'no one killed (only the bugs)'. H. Pinfold also lived near to Holbrooks, at 32 Ashted Row – opposite the 'Workpeoples' Entrance' as it was titled over the door – and similarly brings to mind that night of danger. The sirens wailed at about seven at night and 'we hurried over to Holbrooks with our usual possessions, blankets etc. As my father was on duty fire watching at the factory where he worked, my mother told me to carry my young sister of only a few weeks old in a basket, while she was loaded with our possessions'. The family settled down and 'suddenly we could smell smoke… We realised that Holbrooks was on fire, as Jerry had plastered Holbrooks with incendiary and oil bombs'. The family rushed upstairs and 'what a sight it was that greeted us. Holbrooks was alight from end to end. That was the end of a fine old building that was Holbrooks', and 'the beautiful aromas of vinegar and sauce that used to float our way'.

Cakes and Switzerland: Kunzle's

It wasn't a dream come true. It was another world come true. Never, ever in his most fanciful thoughts had he been able to send his mind soaring to such a place as this, the high peaks of Switzerland. Of course, sometimes he'd come out of the flicks on a Saturday morning and with his pals he'd make out that he was riding the range out in the Wild West. But that was always make believe, he'd been fully aware that it was pretend and that no way could it come true. And yet this was true and it was something that could never even have been hinted at in his imagination. Here he was stood upon the slopes of an Alpine mountain looking down on a deep lake and getting ready to go home to a chateau which rose up romances of knights and ladies, and not of kids from Brummagem.

What a turn up for the book, as his old man would have put it. Him, a back street kid, roaming across meadows which came straight out of the storybook *Heidi* and which were ideal for him and his mates to chase about playing William Tell and Robin Hood all rolled into one. There was no doubt about it, he felt like he'd fell off the top of Rackham's into a new suit. When he'd got here three months ago he'd hardly been able to catch his breath, so bad was his asthma. He'd looked like a little old man, with his shoulders bowled forward, his head lifted to the skies to try and pull in air and his chest and tummy all thin and ribby-looking. What a difference now! Here in the fresh air of eastern Switzerland he'd taken on a new lease of life.

As he'd ceased to fight for his breath, his shoulders had pulled back, his spine had straightened, his head had freed itself from the hold of rasping gasps and his body had filled out. His mom and dad had used to say he looked like a lath. Just wait till they copped sight of him in a few months time when he came home! Wonderful! And to think that such an amazing change had all come about because of the generosity of a Swiss bloke who seemed like Father Christmas, a favourite uncle and a loving grandad all rolled into one. Who was that chap from Switzerland? None other than Christian Kunzle, one of the kindest men ever to walk the streets of Brummagem.

He'd come here in 1903 and straight away opened up a bakery in Snow Hill and a café and shop at 16 Midland Arcade in New Street, where he sold home-made chocolates and cakes. Two years later, the enterprising confectioner started up a branch of his business at 156 Broad Street, between Five Ways and Saint Martin's Street. Soon afterwards, Kunzle's bakery and chocolate making department was moved to a factory just up the road and by the outbreak of the Great War, the company had two more cafés one at 20-21 North Western Arcade and another in Market Street, Leicester. The expansion of Kunzle's continued during the inter-war years and by the late 1920s, the firm not only had a new café in Union Street and an enlarged factory but also it boasted a presence in London, with wholesale showrooms at Charing Cross Road and a café and cake shop in Regent Street.

Despite his interests elsewhere, Christian Kunzle was committed firmly to Birmingham and was deeply concerned with the well being of its citizens. In particular, he was keen to help youngsters and in 1932 he was elected a president of the Children's Hospital in Ladywood. It was this connection which led the philanthropic businessman to make available his family home in Switzerland to poorly youngsters. Chateau Brusselle in Davos was surrounded by 200 acres of park and mountain land and this

Holding his walking stick, Christian Kunzle is in the middle of this photo of the Kunzle's football team. It was taken by Gottfried Rudolf, one of about six apprentices who came with Mr Kunzle from Switzerland and who was involved in opening the original Kunzle factory at Five Ways, Edgbaston. Gottfried met and married his wife at the works and was employed there until he retired aged 70. His daughter, Cynthia M. Jacob, recalls that Mr Kunzle was a good man and that he held a children's party at Christmas and 'we three children used to wait to see what was in the two brown paper carrier bags; a present from Mr Kunzle to us, of a turkey, chocolates, veal, ham pie, Christmas cake and other things!' Before 1939, 'we were only able to visit our Swiss grandparents and many uncles, aunts and cousins the once, and Mr Kunzle paid for our train and boat fare'.

Now aged 86, Edna Bowen was a cleaner at Kunzle's in Union Street and worked from 6 till 8 o'clock in the mornings and in the evenings. Edna actually met Mr Kunzle and his wife 'while I was scrubbing his kitchen floor at a great big house they were moving into'. It was, 'if I remember right, in Richmond Hill Road, Edgbaston – a large detached house. I also was asked if I would like to go to the children's home he had. I was not able to go as I had a young family, but my late mother went instead for a month as she worked for Kunzle's also.' Edna has some very happy memories, especially the tea and concert for wounded soldiers from the war: 'Even the manageress, Miss Webb, did a turn on the stage dressed up. She was dressed in old-fashioned dress and shawl and carrying a bird cage. She sang "My Old Man said Follow the Van".' Betty Benton still has the Kunzle's Handbook of her older sister, Mary Parkes. Mary was at Kunzle's from 1934 until 1959 and Betty has always said 'that no other person had bigger or better chocolate eggs than I with Mary working at Kunzle's and her friend working at Cadbury's!'

feature, allied to a favourable climate, made it a smashing spot for the care of 'debilitated and pre-tuberculous children.'

Before 1939, scores of Brummie kids benefited from the stays in the fresh air and trips resumed again in 1947 when groups of 25-30 youngsters went to Davos on a six months rotation basis. Sadly the visits ended in the mid 1950s following the death of Christian Kunzle. His firm was later absorbed by the Lyons chain but though it is gone, many folk owe their health to the kindness of a Swiss Brummie. And many more of us recall with wistfulness the scrumptious taste of Kunzle's wonderful variety of cakes.

A day out at Barry Island for workers from the cake enrobing department at Kunzle's. Foreman Phil Rose is standing on the left and at the back. Thanks to Alicia Foxall, then Warwick, who went to work at Kunzle's at Five Ways when she was fifteen and had just left school. Alicia suffered from chest trouble and two years after starting at the firm she was sent to Chateau Bruselles to benefit from the Swiss air. The girls she went with had to work whilst they were there, making the beds and cleaning out the dormitories and classrooms – while a couple more would help to serve the meals to the teachers and lads who were in Switzerland because they were asthmatic and had lung trouble. Alicia herself had to keep the living room tidy, but 'after lunch we had the afternoon off to do what we wanted, then they served evening meal and after that, the night was your own'. She was there for a month, unlike the lads who spent between six and twelve months abroad.

Just fifteen at the time, Pauline Langston, née Green, is second from the left in this photo of women making fancy decorations for cakes and other goodies brought out by Kunzle's for Christmas. On her left is Margaret Clark and to her right are Pauline Courtney and Pauline Johnson. Thanks to Pauline Smith. Janet Clark's dad, Frank Killeen made chocolate for Kunzle's cakes and recollects that the famous showboats were made from a chocolate shell which was frozen to the right shape, filled with sponge, covered with cream and finished off with a small, sugar-shaped sweet on top.

Cleaned and Ironed: Laundries

Her mom had always told her, 'As y' mek y're bed y'lie on it', but my oath she'd never med this bed and often she roared deep within herself, 'My God, what ave I done to ave such an ard life!' Mind you, she never let on to the rest of the world how her felt, cus her mother had also drilled into her to 'keep y're troubles to y'rself'. Any road up, it wouldn't have helped if she had gone about bemoaning her lot for there were plenty of others in the same boat or else worse off – and what's more it wouldn't have made things any better. You might have a little blart to yourself behind your net curtains after the kids had gone to bed, but the next day you had to put your nose to the grindstone once again.

That's what her'd done ever since her chap had died leaving her a widow with four little uns. She'd had to push down her grief and hurt and work out how she and the kids were going to survive and stay off the Parish and out of the workhouse. If she'd have had her mom alive or sisters nearby she'd have had someone to mind the kids and would have gone back to pressworking – but that worn't an option. So she did what countless thousands of widows did, she took in washing. She'd traipsed up to Moseley,

This photograph shows the staff who worked at the Co-op Laundry in Bewdley Road, Stirchley in 1940. It was bombed a year later. Beatty (as she was known then) Ellis is fifth from the left on the back row. She met her chap, Jim Hales, at work, for he was a van boy there. Jim notes that after the bombing 'we used to take all the girls in the laundry vans to the Co-op Laundry on the Holyhead Road, Handsworth, every morning. Then we delivered the laundry and picked them back up at night. We did this while the laundry was being rebuilt at Stirchley. It had six bombs dropped on it and was absolutely demolished.' Jim married his sweetheart in 1943 and they have been together for 57 years. Thanks to Jim and Doreen Hales.

This is a cracking shot of the wash-room at the Court Steam Laundry in Bordesley Green. Thanks to Mrs F.E. Hanton. Jane Smith reckons that this was the best of the well-known laundries in Brum. Her mother worked there for years along with two of her daughters, Emily and Irene, and two of her sons, Arthur and Harry, who was a van driver and brother-in-law to the great Brummie music hall artist, Fred Barnes. Jane also recollects the City Steam Laundry in Bloomsbury Street, where she worked and which was owned by her mom's sister. Nellie Pearson (née Bluck) knew the 'Court' well, working there in the 1930s and 40s. Her most vivid memory is of 1941 when 'having spent the night in the Air Raid Shelter, I was cycling to work the next morning along Prince Albert Street, opposite the laundry, and saw many dead bodies, all victims of the night's bombing by the enemy, having dropped a land mine'.

The first memory of Maureen Bartlett (née Bamford) is from about 1942 when her nan, Roseanna Larden, was pushing her in a pram past the 'Mirror' laundry in Sparkhill, in front of which 'was a very high privet hedge'. About six years later, Maureen's mom, Roseanna Bamford, started at the laundry along with her sister Maud Larden. Unsurprisingly, Maureen's first job in 1955 was at the same place, where the manager was Mr Lyons and her immediate boss was Mr Plumpton. There were three other girls in the office, one of whom was May Waite. At that time 'one contract was to wash for the Americans stationed at Banbury. I used to get any buttons or badges and stripes which came off the uniforms. The washing technique hadn't seemed to change much since the time I used to call in and see my mom and auntie on my way home from school. The premises have changed an awful lot now, with separate factories, but Spring Groves Laundries are still going. I've seen their name in the wash room at the NEC on the towel dispensers.'

As a child, Ena Belcher lived in North Road, Harborne, near to the Mirror Laundry in Parkhill Road. At the back of her house was a brook and across it was a field in which Ena and her chums played. They used to climb up the embankment 'to wave to the train driver and from this point we could see the sheets and tablecloths hanging out to dry. They were very white and I wondered how they stayed that way with the trains going past. When the wind was in a certain direction you could smell soap suds and clean washing and quite often there were suds in the brook.'

knocked on the back doors of the posh houses and asked the servants if the family need a washerwoman. Now and then she fell lucky and picked up some work.

Blimey though, it was tough going. The well-off wanted their washing done when they wanted it done and it was useless telling them that she could only have the shared brew'us in the yard once a week. Daily she forced herself out of bed up at five in the morning so as to get in to the wash-house before the woman whose turn it was. She filled the copper, boiled up the laundry, packed the kids off to school, did the maiding, blueing, starching and rinsing, wrung the lot through the mangle she'd bought cheap from the marine store dealer, put the dinner on, pegged out the washing and then ironed it as the hours dragged deep into the night. Often as she stood thumping sheets she'd swear to herself, 'One day, I'll be paying fit, young wenches to do this for me. I'll ave me own laundry, a posh un, with all the proper machines and I'll have drivers to fetch the washing in and tek it back. And I'll pay me workers a fair wage for a fair day's collar.'

With a single-mindedness of purpose and an iron resolve she abarred towards the realisation of her dream. After a couple of years, she'd got enough customers and money coming in to rent a house with its own brew'us. Now she could wash all day long – and because the two big uns picked up the clothes and other things before they went to school, she could take in even more laundry. Soon things were going so well that she was able to take on a couple of women to do the back-wrenching maiding and another one to do the ironing, while she concentrated on making sure that the right washing went back to the right person in the right way.

Gradually her tank of savings grew so's that one day she was able to rent a big, old house. Dilapidated, it had long since been abandoned by the middle class and stood forlorn amidst a sea of back-to-backs, little shops and factories. But for the hard-grafting widow, this house was something special. She did it up, put her and her family on the middle and top floors and turned the downstairs into offices and space for the sorting of the dirty washing after it had been fetched to the premises in big baskets by her collectors. Then she paid for the proper laundry to be built in the large garden at the back.

It had a big, noisy, steamy and wet wash-house, packed with new machinery, a well-laid out ironing room, and a sorting room filled with tables and surrounded by shelves. She was chuffed with everything, but the things she took the most pride in were the calendars, the machines which smoothed the laundry after it had been cleaned. It had been a long struggle, but at last she was no longer a washerwoman, she was the proprietor of a laundry.

Mrs Ellen Randle (known as Nellie) is standing outside Stones's Garden Laundry at 116, Alum Rock Road, Saltley. Thanks to Judy Hanson, the grand-daughter of Nellie, who was the manager at the premises until they were bombed out during the war. It was an agency for Stone's which was based at Goosemoor Lane, Erdington where Cook and Sons now have their furniture store.

Dorothy McEvoy worked at one of the most famous laundries in Birmingham, the Oxford Laundry in Whitmore Road, Small Heath. Its manager was Mr Brown, a well known figure driving a vintage Alvis car and who looked like the colonel off Kentucky Fried Chicken. The laundry was the main point of contact with the Asian immigrants in Small Heath in the early 1960s 'as most of the young men came here single and were living in lodgings and they brought their bundles of washing in along with their problems which the elderly secretary, Mrs Dipple, used to sort out'. The 'Oxford' had a fleet of little electric vans travelling all around Birmingham picking up dirty washing and delivering it washed and ironed three days later. Sadly the business closed 'after the main boiler actually blew up in November 1967'. Nearby in Golden Hillock Road was the Bri Tex Laundry, one of whose famous customer's was Noel Gordon – for whom Dorothy once priced her laundry book.

Violet Tanquee's war-time work was at the Supreme Laundries in the aptly-named Laundry Road, Smethwick, where she washed for the forces and for a 'very large American hospital base stationed at Malvern... plus a large RAF base at Hartlebury with all their washing and an Italian POW camp. The trusted Italians were allowed out of camp to bring their private washes to be laundered, always with an armed guard with a rifle slung over his shoulder – but they were never allowed to speak to us'.

Milk in Bottles: Midland Counties Dairy

Many successful businessmen have boasted that they were self-made men, but there are few whose exploits could have matched those of Edwin White. Born in 1873, he'd started his working life as a farmer's boy. By the time he retired in 1960 aged 87, he was head of the largest private milk distributor and ice-cream company in the country. As chairman of the Midland Counties Dairy Ltd, he oversaw the supply of milk and dairy products to more than three million homes throughout the Midlands. In total, the company distributed a million bottles of milk each day and sold thousands of gallons of ice cream.

How had Edwin White achieved such an outstanding feat? Through hard graft, innovation, principled business dealing, a firm adherence to cleanliness in all food

From left to right these Midland Counties men are Joe Holt, W. Harris and Fred Bowers Senior. Taken in 1920, this was at the old Phillips Street Dairy. Fred Eggison explains that at the turn of the twentieth century, the land in Corporation Street upon which the new Midland Counties Dairy would be built was actually used by a travelling circus – Womble and Bostock – which used to stable its elephants at the back of the 'Old Roebuck' pub on the Aston Road North. Frederick J. Faber actually remembers the origins of the dairy. As a lad of fifteen in 1932, he started work in Moland Street at White's Lemonade Factory: 'it was not a very imposing building. Next to the main gate in Bagot Street was a blacksmith who served the adjacent canal horses and I often in the dinner hour saw these magnificent beasts being shod.' In about 1934, the Whites acquired the adjoining land and bulldozed it clear to make way for the Midland Counties Dairy. Strangely, the first milkmen had to take their milk out in a pushcart and were paid on a commission basis 'not on how many bottles were sold but on how many empties they brought back'.

processing, and an effective partnership with his brother J.G. White. Edwin had entered the dairy trade in a small way, delivering milk to a few customers at three ha'pence a pint. With profits low and the workload heavy, he and his brother moved into a new venture in Chapel Street, Wolverhampton – the selling of ginger beer and herb beer. By 1914 they had also built up a dairy business and had premises in Leicester, Derby, Cardiff, east London, south east London and at Phillips Street, Aston. Still, they had one big worry. In the summer when it was hot, sales of pop were high – but business fell away as the nights drew in, and the cold came.

A Midland Counties Dairy hand cart, early 1920s. Thanks to Mrs D. Timms, whose father, Bill Scaife is holding the cart. He worked for Midland Counties for over 40 years, having come down to Brum from County Durham during the Depression. His doctor had told him to work in fresh air because of his lung problems and so he decided to be a milkman. Ironically, his round was in Smethwick 'which was not exactly a clean air area'. Bill had many T.B. cases on his round and these people would exchange tokens for fresh milk. He used to push his cart fully loaded from the Bearwood Road down to Smethwick Baths, whatever the weather. One of his daughter's earliest memories is of him polishing his leather gaiters ready to wear them the next day 'and I also believe they had to show their hands and nails were clean before setting off'.

Hylda George, née Timms, worked for Midland Counties for 39 years and nine months and they 'were the happiest working days of my life. Mr Edwin White, Mr Jim White, Mr Fred White and Mr M.S. Munro were strict but very fair. They were always available if you had a problem and we had great respect for them. The boss was always particular about the welfare of the horses and about visits from the vet.' Hylda adds that butter was always used in the ice cream – 'I know because our section paid the bills'.

Realising that they needed an operation which had steady sales all the year round, the White brothers re-established firmly themselves in the milk trade. Focusing on Birmingham, they made the crucial decision to avoid the usual practice of retailing milk loose in churns and into which a measure would be dipped so that the liquid could be poured into a bottle, jug or whatever else was brought along by the customer. Thinking this practice unhygienic, the Whites set upon selling milk from sealed bottles. It was a pioneering move which would be followed slowly by their competitors.

This gradual transformation in the attitudes of dairymen was indicative of the importance of the Whites, but they were just as progressive in other ways. Once their business had reached a good turnover and they had sufficient bargaining power, they sought to further ensure the superiority of their product by paying bonuses to farmers who produced milk which was rich in cream and as healthy as possible. By the early 1920s, with the mineral water side of their operations declining, the growing significance of the milk trade was emphasised by the construction of new premises at the bottom of Corporation Street, just before the junction with the Aston Road. Heading a company now known as the Midlands Counties Dairy, the Whites extended their headquarters in the early 1930s and the ongoing growth of their firm was stressed in 1940 by the take-over of the Midland Sterilising Company.

In the years following the end of the Second World War, Midland Counties Dairies continued to expand and did so by adhering to strong principles. Each new worker was given a book outlining the company's Code of Ethics. These enjoined them to deal honestly, obtain business straightforwardly, carry out services ably, act courteously to poor and rich, not make any false statements regarding competitors, and do nothing to bring discredit upon the business. Allied to this code was a powerful commitment to cleanliness. Wash-rooms were installed to encourage employees to scrub their hands regularly and all workers had to wear standard white overalls – while the women among them had their hair gathered up safely and hygienically in a turban.

Such scrupulous standards were as obvious in the preparation of milk for sale. Once the liquid arrived at the dairy, it was tested before it was passed on to homogenisers so that the cream within it could be distributed evenly. The milk was then passed into bottles which had been rinsed, soaked twice in hot soda water, and brushed and scrubbed inside and outside in a great machine capable of cleaning 6,000 bottles an hour. Then, after bottling, the milk was passed on trays through a massive steriliser – the only one of is kind in the world. These wondrous machines can no longer be seen drawing the eyes of onlookers. Like so many other of our outstanding firms, Midland Counties is no more. But yet if it is gone, its codes of practice still call out to us as an example of integrity and fair dealing.

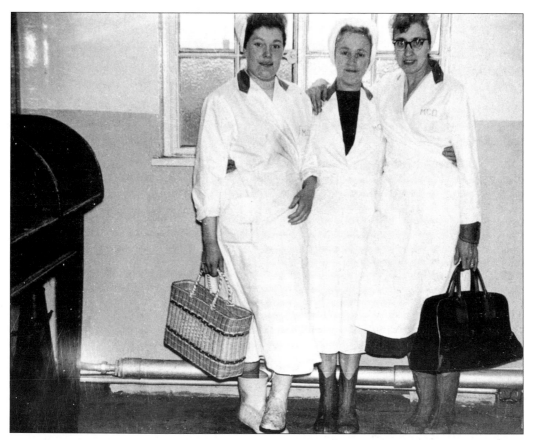

Elsie Milner worked for a few years at the Midland Counties Ice Cream factory, off Corporation Street. It was a good company to work for and all the White family were known as 'Mr John etc., the Mr being before their first names'. This photo shows Elsie on the left with two friends, Lil and Floss, in about 1960. Thanks to Walter Milner During the winter months the women would clean and scrub down the ice cream dairy from top to bottom, including machinery and wagons, trucks, etc. On rare occasions they would go into the milk dairy and help, and 'sometimes they would have to knock the caps on the milk churns to check that the milk was OK before it went into the bottles'.

Flos Summerton, née Green, used to work on the Stera Filling Machine at the Midland Counties Dairy, whilst her husband-to-be Jim Summerton was a dairy mechanic at the firm. He was there for 39 years. Among her own workmates, Flos recalls Harry Harrison, a lovely man 'who loved to bump you with his stomach and say which number machine you were to work'. Then there were Dick Townsend, Albert Jones, Elsie Webb, Nora and Elsie Johnson and Freddy Hobday. On cold mornings, all of them were allowed to pour the boiling hot milk straight from the machines 'into our beakers or cups that were lined up on the cover of the engine that drove the filler. We would use Camp Coffee or cocoa and warm our hands around them.'

Joyce Bassett also met her chap, Ernie, at work. She began at the Midlands Counties in 1938, aged 14. Soon after, when the Blitz on Brum started, she was having to shelter in the stables with the horses. Joyce's father-in-law Bill Bassett 'was there at the very beginning during the First World War when as the White Brothers, the milk bottles were washed by hand in a wash house on Newtown Row'. In such a family-minded business, Joyce made friends like May Dugmore, the O'Connor sisters and Edna Ward.

Making Paper: Smith, Stone and Knight

Day after day, lumbering wagons pulled by heavy horses brought great sacks filled with scraps of material to the paper mills of Smith, Stone and Knight at the Saltley end of Landor Street. As they pulled to a stop in the blue-brick yard, blokes clad in hard-wearing moleskin trousers heaved the bundles over to open-fronted sheds. Their sleeves rolled up almost to their shoulders and their flat caps pushed back to reveal their foreheads, they strained and shoved until the pokes were piled up as far as they'd go without tumbling down. It must have seemed that they laboured in vain, for s'never they'd made one tower it was time to dismantle another and lug the bags outside so's they could be cut open and the bits of this and that strewn on the floor.

That was the signal for the women to get cracking. With blouses buttoned up to their necks and bare arms, they were made more distinctive by the tough urden aprons which covered their frocks. Some had their hair uncovered, others wore strange-looking hats sifted from an old clothes dealer, but most had their locks pulled back and protected by scarves also cut from coarse material. They knew how to collar, did them wenches. Thrusting their hands into the dirty, messy piles they shifted the rags into new mounds according to their type and texture. It was back-bending and neck-stooping work which left their fingers manky with stains from who knows what. That was what was so funny, how those riffy shreds could be turned into something so clean, but that's what happened.

For after they'd been sorted, the rags were taken to be pulped by water, steam and a machine like a meat mincer. Once the rags had been broken down into their basic fibres, the pulp was pumped into storage tanks and then sent on to machines shaped like a big tub. Each contained a drum fitted with blades which turned round and round, so

Women rag sorters at Smith, Stone and Knight, 1890s. Thanks to Smith, Stone and Knight.

The bag making room at Smith, Stone and Knight, 1890s. Thanks to Smith, Stone and Knight. Coming from nearby Cranemore Street in Nechells, John Larner was keen to sign on as an apprentice for Smith, Stone and Knight. Starting at just 14s 8d a week on September 25, 1933, John had to serve six years before he could claim to have learned 'the art, trade or business of paper making'. By the end of his apprenticeship, he was earning £1 17s a week, but within weeks he was called up into Army. After the war, John returned to Smith, Stone and Knight but later went to work as a floater at Mitchell's paper works on the corner of Coventry Road and Watery Lane before returning to his old gaffer at the new mill in his own street.

beating the pulp until its consistency was right and it was ready to be made into paper. Gathered in tanks, water was added to the pulp before it was allowed to run down a chute, through a sieve and onto the paper-making machine. Spread evenly by an apron, the pulp sped along fine-meshed wire which sucked out the water and made it more and more like paper. The stubborn remnants of the liquid were squeezed away between two press rollers after which the product was steam-dried over huge cylinders. If it needed to be made smoother, the paper was pressed by the rollers of a calender and then, at last, it was ready to be cut, checked and gathered in large rolls for sale.

Smith, Stone and Knight weren't the only paper makers in Brum. Amongst the others, Evans and Aldred had a number of works in Birmingham and Smethwick; Broadbent's was in John Bright Street; and both Dickinson and Makin's were in Edmund Street. Then there were Mitchell's, which made fancy paper in Hockley; Tant's, which manufactured crinkled paper in Vauxhall; and Carr's, which formed water-proof paper on Saltley Bridge. And, of course, there was the long-established and well-known Sherbourne Mill of James Baldwin and company at Lifford in Kings Norton. In fact, Thomas Bird Smith of Smith, Stone and Knight was a nephew of James Baldwin and had learned the trade of paper-making whilst working with his uncle.

Funnily enough, neither of his partners had any experience at all of the process. Still, they had set up in 1862, encouraged by the Government's recent decision to drop the duty on the manufacture of paper and also by a growing demand for paper from an increasingly literate population. Beginning with just one machine capable of making no more than six tons of paper a week, the partners and their workers got stuck in. Through a shrewd approach to business and determination, Smith, Stone and Knight soon gained a reputation for fine paper and within a few months, the company had two shifts and had bought a bigger machine. Then in 1873, the decision was taken to build a new mill in Cranemore Street, Nechells. Soon, the firm was also making paper bags and by early this century, it had taken over a business in Bristol as well as the Aston Manor Paper Mills of the Inshaws in Cheston Road. Many of the paper makers of Brum have now gone, but Smith, Stone and Knight continue strongly in business and now lead the way in the recycling of paper.

Mrs Bessie Newey, née Edge, started work at Smith, Stone and Knight when she was fourteen. She was based at Landor Street and made paper bags. Then the firm moved to Crown Road in Bordesley Green. The 'Elite Picture House' was on the corner and the factory was built 'on what was called the Tip'. This photo sent in by Bessie is of a get together of workers and their families in the 1930s. The elderly man in the front row is Syviter Smith, 'The Boss'. In those days 'if we heard he was coming to visit, machines and floors had to be cleaned. Then there was Mr Marshall, he was the manager over us, his son Bob, then Mr Crisp, his son George Crisp.'

Birmingham's Best Bacon: Wrenson's

Can you bring to the fore the days before supermarkets, the days when your mom would do her shopping at a variety of shops – each one of which was a specialist? Can you remember the time when there were thirteen butchers down The Rock, six bread shops down the The Main at Handsworth, five greengrocers on Nechells Park Road, two pork butchers on The Bend at Gooch Street, a pair of confectioners on The Flat at Hockley, a couple of fishmongers on The Cov at Small Heath, a pastry cook in High Street, Erdington, a cooked meat seller on High Street, Aston and a fruiterer on High Street, Deritend? And can you still see in your mind's eye all those grocers who gathered on the Bristol Road as it ran through Bournbrook and Selly Oak?

On the same side as The University of Birmingham there were D. & E. Stores at number 529 and the Maypole Dairy at numbers 615-7, whilst across the flowing traffic were George Mason's at Numbers 628-30 and also at 806. Then there were E. Halward's at number 786, the Ten Acres and Stirchley Co-operative Society at number 830 – and Wrenson's at No 850. It just shows how fast shopping habits have changed when you realise that as late as 1968 there were over 900 separate grocery firms and provision merchants in Brum. This massive number could be swelled even more by the branches of a number of leading grocers. There were the Co-ops, of course, Mason's which had 68 shops in Birmingham, Solihull, Sutton Coldfield and Rubery – with others in Oldbury and Smethwick – and the Maypole which reached 40 outlets in Brummagem alone.

Back in the 1950s there'd been other major grocers, such as the Home and Colonial with its ten stores and Peark's Dairies which had 49 premises, but still there was no doubt as to which grocery business had the biggest presence in our city. It had to be Wrenson's. At its peak, the firm boasted 120 branches. Thirty of the shops were outside Birmingham's boundaries, from Bewdley in the west to Meriden in the east, and from Bloxwich in the north to Stratford-on-Avon in the south. But within Brum it seemed that almost every district had its Wrenson's, often in friendly rivalry with a nearby Mason's.

The business itself had begun in 1909 when nine shops, which had belonged to the wholesale retailer Warriner and Mason, became a private company. These pioneer branches were on the Dudley Road, Winson Green; Ryland Street, Ladywood; Parker Street, Edgbaston; Hingeston Street, Brookfields; King Edward's Road, Ladywood; Bearwood Road, Bearwood; Prince's Corner, Harborne; Prospect Row, Ashted; and Stoney Lane, Sparkbrook. Bar for the last two, all were in western Brum but this confinement to one area was soon ended. Swiftly the company expanded into a city-wide concern and within eleven years it had 40 branches. As it grew, so did its older shops disappear, apart from the one in Hingeston Street, as the focus was shifted to premises on main shopping thoroughfares.

Wrenson's was a clear success story, much of which was due to its General Manager, Henry Carlin. He came from a family of Cannock grocers and had managed one of the original Wrenson's stores before the company was formed. His trading beliefs were encapsulated in two words: 'Quality and Service'. These principles were

The Billesley branch of Wrenson's on the Yardley Wood Road where Ken Elcock was manager from 1949. Ken, who sent in this photo, worked for Wrenson's for over 30 years, starting as an errand boy at the Kings Heath branch when he was fourteen in 1932. He has no doubt that his employers sold the best provisions money could buy, such as Danish tub butter, Canadian cheddar cheese which would melt in your mouth, lovely English lard and the finest smoked bacon from Wiltshire. One Christmas Eve, just before the war, it was 11 o'clock at night and the manager, Mr Turner, went to the front of the shop, stood on the step, came back in and said, 'I don't think we will shift just yet as there are still a few people about. We might sell that last Christmas cake.' Ken eventually got home about midnight: 'I was crackered. And we never did sell that Christmas cake!'

Beryl Robins worked for Wrenson's for nine years from 1945. At first, she did simple accounts related to each shop, of which there were then 99 then, and was taught to operate a National Accounting Machine. Soon after, Beryl was moved to the Reception Office which included the Switchboard 'which I loved', and 'meeting everyone on their arrival and conversing with the shop managers and reps who visited the company'. Wrenson's was a very good firm to work for and working conditions were excellent. There were two generous bonuses each year, the free lunches were excellent ('the dining table was the longest I have ever seen') and there was an annual works outing to London, on which everyone was taken free of charge.

Margaret Haddon was seventeen when she started work for Wrensons and explains that the name came from an amalgamation of Warriner and Mason's, the food suppliers with which Wrensons was involved. She was employed in a corner shop with a counter service and a wooden chair 'in which some of the customers would sit for hours gossiping about something while I was rushing about putting their order'. The customers became so well-known that they were like family members and 'we had a book where we would enter credit for those paying at the end of the week'. Margaret especially loved the Christmas atmosphere as 'everyone was cheerful and happy as the season got into full swing'. She worked for Wrenson's for three years and will never forget the great experience.

held as firmly by Moss and Mendel Mindelsohn. They joined the business as directors in 1920 and with Carlin guided the progress of Wrenson's. Together they made it possible for a customer to pass an order book into any branch for immediate attention and quick delivery. Together they gained the reputation that Wrenson's bacon was unsurpassed. And together they proclaimed that theirs was 'a business in Birmingham for Birmingham people, by Birmingham people'.

David A. de Saxe is standing talking to one of the Wrensons deliverymen at the start of the Outer Circle convoy. An executive member of the company's board of directors, David, who sent in this photo, worked at Wrensons from 1957 until 1971. A cousin of the one-time chairman, Keith Mindelsohn, David organised this publicity stunt in the early 1960s when he was Transport Director. After obtaining police permission, he arranged for over 30 Wrensons delivery vans to drive in convoy in an anti-clockwise direction around the Outer Circle Number 11 Bus route. The delivery vans were resplendent in the blue and cream livery of Wrensons – as were the firm's about 200 bicycles.

David stresses that these latter played a significant role in keeping up Wrensons famed reputation for its delivery service and were maintained by Chris Ford, a centrally-based cycle mechanic. The bicycles were made by Grundles, another old Birmingham company, whilst the vans were chain-transmission Trojans. Gradually, the vehicles were replaced from 1955 by Bedfords, each of which bore across its scuttle the slogan 'Birmingham's Best Bacon' with a dancing pig at each end.

Vic Secker stresses the the importance of this slogan and of two others: 'Wrensons Service' and 'There's a Wrensons round the corner ready to serve you'. Several streets and roads had two branches, Erdington High Street had three, and no branch was more than 25 miles from the head office: 'Family grocers we were, and one big happy family at that, as our wives and children in a lot of cases were known to supervisors and directors'. In 1962, Vic received a cup from Mr Mindelsohn for managing the best branch.

Staff at Wrenson's, Acocks Green Village on the corner of Dudley Park Road and the Warwick Road. Third from left is Frank Hatton, manager of the store from 1934 to 1971, and second from the right is his wife Phyllis. Thanks to R. Hatton, who lived above the store from when he was two in 1934 until he married in 1957. Standing to the right of Phyllis is Leslie G. Roberts. It was his first job after leaving school and he was fifteen when this photo was taken. Although, he was only at the branch for about twelve months, Leslie enjoyed every minute and used to make more money in tips delivering groceries on the carrier bike than he earned in wages. He was devastataed when he had to give in his notice on the orders of his father 'due to the fact that I ran out of dry clothing on a particularly inclement day'.

This commitment to the city meant that the company was run on family lines even after it became a public company, so that wherever possible appointments were made from within the firm. Such a commitment was matched by the loyalty of the staff, many of whom remained with Wrenson's for most of their working life. Like the other grocers of Old Brum, Wrenson's is no more – but I bet many of us can still smell their bacon and taste their tea.

Mrs L.R. Tredwell's husband Tom started with Wrenson's in 1928 and five years later became the manager of the Birchfield Road shop, after which he moved to the premises on the Dudley Road. It was a 'really, happy family business and we were treated well by Mr Carlin, the managing director'. Mrs Tredwell especially recollects how shop work was so different to what it is today, and how hard the errand boys worked, 'with their bicycles piled up with grocery'.

Mrs D. Harper used to live near the Wrenson's on the corner of Arthur Road and Grove Lane, Handsworth, and he recalls vividly the bacon which hung from the ceiling on hooks, the sugar which was weighed and served from sacks and the cheese which still had the rind on and was cut with wire. In fact, Mrs Harper still has an old Wrenson's Order Book from the 1950s in which 1lb of marg was 2s 6d, lb of tea was 3s 2d, a packet of Oxo was 9d, a block of cooking salt was 7d and a tin of salmon was 7s 6d. David Mellon worked for Wrensons for 22 years. He stresses the importance attached by the firm's directors to serving the customers well and efficiently and adds that it was a pleasure 'to go to work for such a company as they showed the same concern for staff as customers'. David was also sports and social secretary for Wrensons and organised three dances a year for the staff. For him, Wrensons was 'a company from the top down that showed that working together in a family atmosphere created the customer confidence that is not so readily seen these days'.

Chapter 4:

Sights, Sounds and Smells
of Old Brum

Gymnasts and Lion Tamers: The Circus

He was one of the most well-known circus artistes of the age, famed for his gymnastics and feted for his daring – and he was Brummagen bred and born. His name? Well, in the circus he was known as the Great Leno. But in the run-up to the Christmas of 1858, he'd been christened the more prosaic Harry Brooks. Little is known about his early life, but he was just ten years old when he was apprenticed to a pair of gymnasts called Sipple and Dickens, who were appearing at the Curzon Hall in Suffolk Street. Later the site of the 'West End' Picture House and Ballroom, Curzon Hall had been opened as recently as 1865. Constructed at a cost of about £7,500 for the purposes of dog shows, it had a capacity of 3,000 people and soon it became a major centre for exhibitions, panoramas, entertainments and circuses.

What made young Harry's mom and dad let him be apprenticed we don't now, but it was a period when times were hard for working folk and many youngsters were out collaring from the ages of six and seven. Whatever the case, not long after joining the circus, Harry was on his way to Europe where he learned his trade, travelling from town to town. Still only a kid, he gained a reputation for his gymnastics on the rings and horizontal bars – but all that traipsing around the Continent started to get on his nerves. So, with his apprenticeship served, Harry decided to come back to Britain to join John Swallow's tenting show which was touring Scotland.

Leaving that company, the young Brummie then teamed up with a trick cyclist known as Stirk. It was during this partnership that 'Harry' dropped his name and instead took for himself the moniker of 'Leno'. It was an appropriate choice for in France 'leno' signified an open-work fabric in which the warp threads were twisted in pairs before weaving. Mind you, Leno nearly didn't have a pairing. Showing off their skills at Plymouth, he and his partner were flung into the orchestra pit when the wheels of the cycle they were riding slipped. With smashed musical instruments littered about them, Leno and Stirk were lucky to get away without serious injury.

Not surprisingly, the two blokes decided to go their own ways and Leno took up with two other circus artistes, Lerroux and Ferdinand – the most noted clowns and vaulters of the day. Once again Europe beckoned and for five years Leno was away from home. When he came back again, it was to work first with Hengler's Circus in Liverpool and then at Newsom's Hippodrome in his hometown of Brum. Next followed a stint with Lord George Sanger's company and visits to Austria and Germany, and for the last time Leno caught the boat back to England, on this occasion to Blackpool. That was in 1881 and it was now that the well-travelled gymnast developed both a flying trapeze act and a dramatic role, playing the 'hero' in 'Dick Turpin's Ride to York'.

The acts proved a great success and by 1883 Leno had become a household name in the North West, where audiences thrilled to his tumbles, his rides, his leaps over horses and his agility in the aerial trapeze. Still, it was a dangerous game and during one show in Oldham, the bar on the double trapeze gave way. In those days there were no safety nets and Leno fell to the ground. He was rushed to hospital and during his

Circus elephants going past Bedder's Fish and Chip Shop on their way to the recreation ground in Hay Mills. This photograph was taken by the husband of Mrs E.J. Busby.

W.E. Perks has an early memory of Bostock and Wombell's show on the Sandpits site in about 1926. There was also Bronco Bill's Circus at Berkeley Road East, Small Heath in 1928. The principal owner was John Swallow – interestingly the same man, or the son of the bloke, for whom the Great Leno worked in the 1870s. Swallow had two elephants, Salt and Saucy: 'I well remember the closing act. It consisted of riders dressed as cowboys and Indians. The Indians attacking the stagecoach with the cowboys coming to the rescue. It was bloodthirsty acting.' The next circus was that of Bartram Wills on the Heybarnes Recreation Ground and 'what wonderful shows they put on'. Then there were the circuses at Bingley Hall and Aston Hip, as well as Rosaire's Circus and Billy Kaye's Circus at the Serpentine in Aston.

A poster for William Cooke's Circus at Bingley Hall in 1853. Thanks to Kerry Foley who performs as Kavanna, the ultimate speciality act. When Jo Gaskin was born in 1925, her mom and dad, Doll and Bill Praed, travelled with Pat Collins's Circus. Bill was a juggler, 'but what or whoever you were, everyone had to work to hoist the big top... In those days we had horse drawn caravans, as a family of five we had two, with a big horse and a smaller one. I have never forgotten the scent of the wood kindling as we sat round the camp fire. The music of violins, harmonicas and piano accordions played by the true Romanies. Their children with black, ringleted hair dressed with red ribbons contrasted with my hair, white and straight. I watched the clowns and artsits practice. I remember still the feel of sawdust or straw under my bare feet and the sounds and smells of the amminals.' Eventually, Jo's family settled down and later had a shop in Monument Road and worked at the 'Crown Cinema' in Icknield Port Road.

convalescence fell in love with his nurse, a Miss Crompton, whom he later married. Not long after this event, Leno left the circus and changed back to Henry Brooks.

After a spell running a pub in Blackpool, he was appointed as the managing director of the Alhambra Company, which had just put up a row of buildings opposite the Tower. The development included a variety theatre, ballroom, cafe, billiard saloon, roof gardens, shops and, of course, a circus. This was opened on Whit Monday 1899 by Mrs Dudley Smith, the daughter of George Kynoch who'd started the munition works in Witton, Birmingham. The 'Alhambra' later became the 'Palace', whilst Henry moved into politics. As a leading councillor, he was voted Mayor of Blackpool for two years until 1924. A year later, as chairman of the borough's electricity committee, Henry Brooks made a major impact upon the town of his adoption when he pioneered the first illuminations. So next time you gaze in delight at the lights in Blackpool – remember, without a Brummie they might never have been turned on.

I'd like to thank Mrs Rita Hall of West Heath for sending me information on Harry Brooks, the Great Leno.

The lion tamer is Captain Bill Howes, a distant uncle of John F. Humphries. The backdrop suggests that the lion tamer is on a stage and John thinks that he is performing at the Aston Hippodrome in the 1950s. John saw his uncle at this venue and tells me that sadly, Captain Howes' son was later killed by a lion. L. Johnson was Sid Howes' cousin and recalls that Sid had it very hard, as did the rest of the family. At one time he lived with his parents in Colville Road, Sparkbrook but tragically both of them died within a couple of weeks of each other. Sid had to go into the Shenley Fields Home as his gran was already looking after one her sons who had been crippled in the war and was a widower with two children. Later in life, Sid was in a film with Lilian Harvey. Photograph thanks to Alfred Orson.

Len Layton recalls that his old mom wouldn't let her kids go to the circus because they couldn't afford it, and because the lions had escaped some years before at the Onion Fair on the Serpentine Ground. Yet Len did get to see the animals 'as they used to be stabled at the top of St Clement's Road by the railway. The owner was Mr Derby, a friend of my dad's, and he would send us to fetch manure for his roses.' In 1930, Flo Naylor's Dad was going to take her and a young cousin to the circus in the Sandpits, but before they went the Big Top was destroyed by fire. A lion tamer risked his life by going into the lion's cage and treating them for burns. A new marquee was erected, but that night a heavy snow storm snapped the poles 'so once again we were disappointed. However, the circus moved to a hall in West Bromwich and Dad took us there on the Saturday.' The man who saved the lions was George Kulovits, a legendary star of the circus, who performed under the name of Tagore. Born in Hungary, he was appearing with Carmo's Circus and for his bravery he was presented with a commemorative ring by the Lord Mayor of Birmingham.

Succouring the Sick: Dudley Road Hospital

She seemed a forbidding figure with her lips pulled together seriously and a gaze that was resolute and firm. That solemn look was heightened by her long, black frock and the stiffly starched cuffs of her sleeves and it was reinforced by her purposeful, strong walk. There was no doubt about it, she was a determined and robust character, but from closer up it became obvious that her strength was tempered by gentleness. Her hands lay clasped easily above her waist, there was a tender tinge in her eyes and she made you feel that she cared. And Anne Gibson certainly did care, she cared deeply about helping others.

Miss Ann C. Gibson, matron of Birmingham Infirmary. Thanks to City Hospital. Mrs Betty Collings recalls another important matron. Betty began her nursing training at Dudley Road Hospital in March 1948 under the 'matronage' of Miss Birtwistle. She was an awe-inspiring woman 'but the system was really first rate and we learned.' Win Francis was also in training as a nurse at the hospital between 1948-51. They were happy years as they were for many young ladies and the occasional man from all over Britain and from Ireland, Holland, Malta and Germany. There was even one nurse from Abyssinia, who after training as an SRN and midwife was to return to set up a maternity hospital: 'The work was hard, the hours were long and the discipline was very strict but we became some of the best-trained nurses in the world. Yes the world because many of our nurses went on to work in other countries. I had one friend who went on to train as a missionary in Thailand or Siam as it was then. Others returned to their own countries, spreading the name of D.R.H. far and wide. We saw many changes in treatment because of the revolution in new medicines. To see young people with T.B. who in the past would have died of the disease, getting better because of streptomycins and its allied medicines was nothing short of a miracle!' Mrs H. Turner worked as an auxiliary at Dudley Road Hospital from the 1950s until her retirement in 1986. She remembers the Archway of Tears. There was a legend of the ghost of a grey-caped lady who would be seen by nurses on night duty. Each Christmas 'we used to walk through to All Saints and were given a lovely lunch and we even had coach trips to the country'.

Raised in Edinburgh, she entered the Nightingale School for nurses in 1881 and after her 12 months' training was appointed assistant to Mary Cadbury at the Liverpool Infirmary. That member of the famed chocolate-making family later moved to the Queen's Hospital in Bath Row, but it was as matron of the Birmingham Infirmary that Anne Gibson herself was to become best known. She took up her appointment in January 1889 and the *Nursing Record* congratulated the authorities 'upon their good fortune in having secured such valuable services'. Soon after, her assistant wrote to their mentor, Florence Nightingale, and explained that Miss Gibson had done wonders.

Nurses and patients in Dudley Road Hospital. This photograph was taken between 1923 and 1926 by Mr W.E. Gregory, an X-Ray porter. Thanks to City Hospital. This remarkable man was Bill Gregory's Dad. An engineer at Longbridge before 1914, he contracted malaria during the war and could not work near machinery again. After he was demobbed, he was unemployed for a while until 1921 when he obtained a job as a porter at Dudley Road Hospital. A man who was naturally technically minded, Mr Gregory was soon involved in the early X-Ray Department. He wore a rubber suit, lead boots and rubber gloves and he and a colleague would hold metal rods which were attached to the X-Ray machines. They would walk towards each other and when the electricity flashed across the four to five feet gap between the rods the power was correct for the required X-Ray depth. Mr Gregory also took photos of patients' problems, which Bill passed on to Dudley Road Hospital. In later years, Mr Gregory became a mortuary attendant 'and again for many years dealt with the job precisely. He was the first person to remove a spine intact and this was used in lectures at Birmingham University'; and he brought the NUPE union to the hospital.

The Infirmary itself was as new as its matron. Costing well over the huge sum of £100,000, it was a building erected on the grand scale. Its kitchens had immense steam and gas ranges in which could be cooked three hundredweight of meat, a hundred gallons of gruel, three sacks of potatoes and 60 gallons of tea; its steam laundry could cope with the washing, wringing, mangling and ironing of 20,000 articles each week; its wards, if placed end to end, would make a passage a mile long; and its staircases, if put one on top of the other, would reach 1,000 feet and loom over the Eiffel Tower.

In total there were four residents and two visiting medical officers, a large staff of men and women who carried out domestic and administrative duties, and 79 nurses. They cared for anything between 1,110 and 1,600 patients – all of whom were very poor. For this infirmary belonged to the dreaded workhouse in Winson Green, just off the Dudley Road. It had been built in a belated acknowledgement that it was not the fit who sought help from the authorities but rather the elderly, the infirm and the sick.

Mrs M. Quittenden and her husband were active members of the Dudley Road Hospital League of Friends and for the November 1967 Christmas Fayre they asked 'The Pearly Kings and Queens' to open the event. This photo sent in by Mrs Quittenden shows two of the Pearly Queens at the bedside of a patient and alongside them are the matron and Lord Mayor of Birmingham.

Betty Mattiello recalls that when her dad was in B8 Ward no-one could visit him without a pass, which Betty still has. It's dated October 17, 1946, addressed to Mrs Higgins of New Canal Street. Mrs Layton was nine when she was taken to Dudley Road with peritonitis. She came into a startling white world, 'nurses with brilliant white starched uniforms, bed sheets everywhere gleaming with polish and shining like a new pin'. Mrs Layton has no doubt about the importance of Dudley Road: 'I owe my life to a great hospital and staff'.

And when these folk called for assistance from the Infirmary then they had to come through the Archway of Tears to be seen by a workhouse doctor and formally admitted. Then they would be taken to the receiving house of the Infirmary itself where their clothes would be taken from them and they would be given the garb of the institution. Those with a disease like scarlet fever would be sent to the nearby City Infectious Hospital; those with a contagious disease like opthalmia would be taken to a detached ward of the infirmary; and those in other categories would be placed in either a medical or surgical ward – according to whether they were men, women or children.

Despite its connection with the loathed workhouse, the Birmingham Infirmary soon became a vital place of support for those who were poverty-stricken in Old Brum. Increasingly, it came to have an independent existence, a shift that was passionately supported by Anne Gibson. She was avowed in her intent to turn the Infirmary into a place more like a hospital, 'where nurses are given their proper position, as well as fed, taught and housed as in any hospital'.

Anne Gibson retired in 1912. It was under the care of her successor, Marion Thomas, that the Birmingham Infirmary finally made the shift into a true general hospital. That move was impelled by Dr. F.W. Ellis. He opened the Infirmary to all people requiring urgent medical attention. In the process he turned the Infirmary into the Dudley Road Hospital – now the City Hospital. Its doctors, nurses, auxiliaries, porters, cleaners, clerics and staff of all kinds carry on the traditions instilled by Anne Gibson and Dr Ellis. They succour the ill, they care for the poorly, they treat the unwell and they bring comfort to the ailing.

We Shall Remember: The Hall of Memory

That summer's day, June 12, 1923, thousands of ex-servicemen walked solemnly towards the junction of Broad Street and East Row. Wearing their best suits, with their boots blacked and polished and with their medals pinned proudly to their chests, they presented a disciplined and military look despite their civilian clothes. They were joined by hundreds upon hundreds of relatives of those who had died in the First World War. Many were women weeping silent tears – some of whom were still dressed in the black of mourning – while others were youngsters determined to stand with backs straight and stomachs pulled in so as to honour properly their loved ones who had fallen.

The opening of the Hall of Memory in July 1925. Thanks to the Birmingham <u>Evening Mail</u>. The Lord Mayor of Birmingham, Alderman Pervical Bower, is in the middle of the photo and he's talking to the uniformed Prince Arthur of Connaught. Suzanne Scott still has her late mother's programme for the opening. It was a much-treasured possession because Suzanne's mother had lost her eldest brother in the First World War. His name was G.W. Carter of the Post Office Rifles and he was just 21 when he was killed in 1917. For many years, Suzanne's mother visited the Hall of Memory 'and I have gone in there to look at my uncle's name. I have also visited his grave four times in Belgium, along with the graves of my father's two brothers who were killed in 1917 and 1918. They are commemorated in Scotland.' Suzanne has no doubt that the Hall of Memory is a marvellous building which must always stand in remembrance 'of the young men and women who gave their lives often at such a young age for their country'.

From all over Birmingham they came to a spot which had recently been cleared of the premises of Southall Bros and Barclay Limited, chemical apparatus manufacturers, and a number of small shopkeepers such as Abram Abrams the tailor and Charles Hector the second-hand bookseller. This large assembly had come to remember those who had fallen in the war and that never would they forget. The stillness of the crowd was remarkable for its great size, and it remained a dignified and grave congregation throughout the ceremony – throughout which everyone was focused upon the slight figure of His Royal Highness, Edward, Prince of Wales.

He took hold of a silver trowel and an ivory mallet so that he might lay the foundation stone for what was to be the Hall of Memory. Both tools were beautifully designed and executed by Bernard Cuzner and others at the Central and Vittoria Schools of Art. As the Prince held the trowel and mallet, he declared that the Memorial would stand 'to symbolise to generations to come all that Birmingham stood for during a period of great national crisis – work of every kind unflinchingly given, compassion to the sick and wounded, courage and resources in adversity, and, above all, self sacrifice, dedicated as it was to the immortal memory of the heroic dead'.

There is no doubt that Brummies had played their part to the full in the Great War. From the lads at Austin to the wenches at the BSA, the city's workers had turned out the

Part of the large congregation at the Service of Thanksgiving for victory in Europe at the Hall of Memory on May 9, 1945. Thanks to the Birmingham <u>Evening Mail</u>.

munitions so vital to victory. And Brummie blokes had answered the call to arms. Over 150,000 of them had seen service. Sadly, 35,000 of those men were wounded and 12,320 killed. The people of Birmingham were resolved that these men would not be forgotten. Nor were they. Through a public subscription, Brummies raised over £60,000 for the clearance of the site and the building of the Hall of Memory.

The demolition of the old buildings was actually carried out by Martin Ciangretta, an Italian Brummie who had lost a son in the war, while the hall itself was designed by S.N. Cooke and W. Norman Twist. It was built by John Barnsley and Sons, mostly employing local men. Construction was finished in 1925 and on July 4 that year, the Hall of Memory was opened by His Royal Highness Prince Arthur of Connaught. Once again, a huge crowd assembled to pay their respects at a building 'erected to the glory of God and in memory of the men and women of this city who fell in the Great War'.

Octagonal in shape, the Hall of Memory is flanked by four bronze statues carried out by Albert Toft to symbolise the contribution made to the war by the Navy, Army,

Miss Marjorie Summerfield, of Bournville, in 1988 stands in front of the Hall of Memory's Roll of Honour, to which her father's name had recently been added in a simple ceremony of dedication carried out by the Lord Mayor of Birmingham, Councillor Harold Blumenthal. Her Dad was Private Leo Horton Summerfield of the 6th Battalion the Royal Berkshire Regiment and he was killed in battle in France on October 21, 1917. Thanks to the Birmingham <u>Evening Mail</u>.

Air Services and Women. Inside is a shrine which supports a bronze casket. Within it lies a magnificently inscribed and illuminated Roll of Honour designed by Sidney Metyard of the Birmingham Central School of Art. On the walls are three reliefs which indicate different aspects of the Great War. The first shows men leaving home to join up and it records the number of Brummie servicemen who were killed or disabled. The second depicts a party of men in the firing line and bears the powerful words, 'At the going down of the sun and in the morning we shall remember them'. The third portrays the wounded and maimed coming home. It states simply yet movingly, 'See to it that they shall not have suffered and died in vain'.

Two wreaths were also placed inside the Hall of Memory. Both were presented by the town of Albert in France. They read 'to the children of Birmingham who fell in the cause of right and liberty from the people of Albert in gratitude'. Let us pray to God there will be no more children of Birmingham who will lose their lives in war. And when we pass the Hall of Memory, let us not rush past but let us stop and go within to bow our heads and honour those who paid the ultimate price for freedom. We shall remember.

Saturday Treat: The Market Hall

It was Thursday February 16, 1835 and it seemed as if every Brummie had made their way to the historic heart of the town. Down High Street they came and up Digbeth they

The Bull Ring entrance of the Market Hall on a quiet day in the early 1900s. Mrs Eileen Smith is now 85 and well remembers the posh entrance of the Market Hall and its wooden rail which ran down its steps for the 'up and down shoppers'. She loved Saturdays, for on that day it was her weekly treat to be taken on the tram to the Bull Ring – and the Market Hall was their first call. Just inside was a huge sweet stall 'where every Saturday my dad bought me $\frac{1}{2}$ lb sweet fishes – they were about 2" long so lasted nearly a week! It was so noisy with all the men shouting to buy theuir crocks, meat, vegetables and flowers.' Bill Drew also has happy memories of the old Market Hall. As a lad in the 1930s, he was taken there by his dad and recalls that people used to gather around the clock to see the figures strike the time. Bill's dad used to enjoy all the sea food on sale in the Market Hall, but his favourite was jellied eels whilst Bill loved whelks or mussels. Above all 'there was an atmosphere about the place we both enjoyed'.

Jean Perks is another person with memories of that wonderful clock: 'How I would love to stand in the crowd and wait for the chimes when the figures moved,' she says. 'Then there were all the pet stalls, with cages containing puppies, kittens, rabbits and other animals.' When Jean was about seven, her Dad took her to the Market Hall where 'to my delight he bought me a black and white mongrel pup – which we named Bob'. Now aged ninety-three, Mary Geddes also has a vivid recollection from her childhood of an old chap who stood in the gutter at the bottom of the steps to the Market Hall. Swaying from side to side, he used to call out in a sing-song voice: 'Sewing needles, dashing needle and bodkin, a penny the whole lot'.

traipsed. And all with one aim – they wanted to gaze in awe at the new Market Hall. The crowds were as great the next day and again on the Saturday – swelled as they were by the country folk from outlying villages and hamlets. Rich and poor, old or young – it mattered not a jot. All were united in their praise of this spectacular building which was the pride of the Bull Ring.

Little wonder that it drew such notice, for it was the newest, biggest and most impressive public structure in the whole of Birmingham. What a sight it was to behold! There it stood, 365 feet in length, 180 feet wide and 60 feet high. With such dimensions, it dominated the landscape at the bottom of the High Street, stretching as it did all the way to Worcester Street and virtually filling the whole of the space between Bell Street and Philips Street. But it wasn't only the size of the Market Hall which drew the breath of onlookers and had folk shaking their heads in amazement. This building wasn't just large, it was also grand.

It had two main entrances in High Street and Worcester Street, and impressively both were flanked by two mighty Doric columns. Behind them were massive archways and above them were elegant porticoes. Large yet graceful, the structure looked as if it had been transplanted from ancient Athens into the midst of industrial Brum. The vast majority of folk had seen nothing like it, for no other building in Birmingham shouted out so loud a bond between one of the world's greatest manufacturing towns and the greatest city state of Classical Greece.

Of course, within a few years Brummies would get used to that look, what with the Town Hall and the hotel at Curzon Street Railway Station. But for now, that kind of structure was fresh, inspiring and breathtaking. If anything, it was even more so after the gloaming had faded into evening. For then the interior of the Market Hall was lighted with gas for the benefit of traders and shoppers alike.

In all there were 600 odd stalls 'fitted up for the sale of fruit, game and poultry, fish, butcher's meat, fancy articles, live pets, etc.' For the next 100 years and more, traders continued to sell the same goods and Brummies carried on flocking to the Market Hall. Then in 1936, the building was enhanced with a fascinating feature which appealed to both youngsters and their moms and dads. It was a beautiful clock which boasted three bells, the largest of which weighed three hundredweight. Upon the hour and the half hour, these bells were struck by one of four solid oak figures – three of which were medieval knights and one of which was a damsel. Originally placed in the Imperial Arcade in Dale End in 1883, the clock stopped ticking and striking after twenty years. Then in the mid-1930s 'Our' Percy Shurmer, the chairman of the council's Markets' Committee, had the clock repaired and brought to the Market Hall where it became the biggest attraction throughout the markets complex.

The figure and two of the bells were destroyed on the night of August 25, 1940 when German bombers dropped a high explosive and incendiaries on the Market Hall. Fortunately the attack took place on a Sunday and there was only one person in the building. He was the night-watchman, Mr V. Letherington, and before he made his escape he bravely unlocked the cages containing animals and released them to escape through the swing doors into the street. A few days later the scene at the Market Hall was described by a reporter. The structure was a roofless shell, filled with blackened and charred beams of wood. On one wall was an opening, across which was put a barrier. The other side was a mass of rubble, pieces of iron, bricks and a few utensils.

A lone ARP volunteer stands amidst the wreckage of Birmingham's Market Hall on August 26, 1940. Thanks to the Birmingham <u>Evening Mail</u>. Thelma Coulson can only remember the Market Hall without its roof. Each Saturday she and her mom would walk through the building on their way to their bus in Navigation Street. They entered up the steps from the Bull Ring, 'past the lady who shouted 'andy carrier, 'andy carrier, selling those bags made of thick brown paper with string handles'. After spending some time by the pet stalls, Thelma and her mom would go to the shop that sold 'those lovely sugar fish – a taste never quite recaptured'. Then it was on to the Fish Market, 'avoiding being splashed with water as the counters were washed down, where we purchased crabs' claws for Dad and a bag of winkles for us'. Thelma's mom always kept a couple of safety pins under the lapel of her coat so that they could take the eye of the winkle 'and tease the delicacy out of its shell' so that the pair of them could tuck into their feast at the back of the bus.

As a child, Brian Henderson's attention was the goldfish stall, from which were also sold domestic fowl chicks. Then there was the 'infamous 1,000lb German bomb, Satan, which had devastated the bottom end of New Street and which was relocated to the Market Hall from the Big Top site'. But Brian's most evocative memory is of one dark evening after the shopkeepers and stallholders had gone. Walking up the Bull Ring 'I could see along Bell Street and the gas-lit street lamp outside a pub, which had leaded windows. It was just like a scene from a Dickens novel. As the mist drifted through the yellow light I imagined I had stepped back in time. However, the bus I got on to go home was not pulled by a horse.'

Only the iron frames of the stalls remained identifiable. On Albert Pope's had been struck two small Union Jacks and on Yates's had been scrawled the defiant words, 'Burnt but not broke.'

After the war the Market Hall, still with no roof, was re-opened and once again it drew in Brummies. What a pity it was not restored to its full splendour. Instead in 1963 it was closed and then knocked down. Now that the Bull Ring is to be redeveloped with a new Market Hall what a thing it would be if we had a cracking clock to stare at as once we had.

The old Market Hall lies forlorn and awaits its demolition as the new Saint Martin's Queensway wraps round it and turns it into an isolated island. The Worcester Street entrance has been knocked down already, whilst Bell Street has disappeared to the left of the Market Hall and the Fish Market has gone with it. The triumph of new Birmingham is made plain by the the new buildings flanking Smallbrook Street in the background. To the right of the Market Hall, the remnant of Phillips Street is dotted with the cars which will lead to the wide dual carriage ways which swept away so much of Old Brum. Thanks to the Birmingham Evening Mail.

Tolkien's Land: Sarehole Mill

When the moon is full and the sky is clear, traipse slowly down Green Road, Moseley towards the ford of the River Cole. Just before the gently flowing brook, slip through the entrance of the rec and stand awhile in front of the palings so that your eyes can take in the full beauty of the sight before you. There, silhouetted by the lunar glimmer, stands the seemingly enchanted chimney and buildings of Sarehole Mill. Then walk steadily across the park and climb the little slope to the fencing by the side of the mill. Here above a short stream floats a great pond, hemmed in by thick foliage, overhung by stretching trees and lit up by the shimmering glow of the moon. Strangely quiet Canadian Geese hop along the narrow banks, while mallards smoothly glide across the almost still water.

Now close your eyes. Occasionally the rumble of the city pushes through the silence, but mostly it feels as if you've leaped back to the time when Sarehole was a hamlet distant from Brum, when kingfishers flew freely above the fields of Swanshurst Farm and when youngsters fished for jack bannocks in the Coldbath. It's as if you're

Loading sacks of flour at Sarehole Mill, about 1891. The bearded man on high is looking towards Colebank Road. Is he one of the Andrew brothers and perhaps the 'white ogre' who shooed Tolkien from his land 15 years later? Thanks to Birmingham Museums Services.

A view of Sarehole Mill from the Wake Green Road. Thanks to the Birmingham <u>Evening Mail.</u> John Sharpe has always been enchanted by Sarehole Mill, even as a lad when it lay in ruins, and he has written a poem which captures his fascination both for the building and the books of Tolkien. It is called 'The Hobbits of Sarehole Mill'

From willow tree at Sarehole Mill, the trilling blackbird greets the day,
'tis here just when the sun comes up that Tolkien's hobbits quietly play.
Beside the ivy covered mill 'midst waving grass and rushes tall,
If you stand there and close your eyes I'm sure you'll hear a hobbit call.
And as the rising sun comes up with shining rays across the skies,
by strange chance if you are there I know you'll hear a hobbit cry.
If you should look across the pool and see the mute swan gently glide,
you may make out upon his back a hobbit on his morning ride.
And where the bluebells gently sway when all is quiet and still about,
just listen on the gently breeze, I'm sure you'll hear a laugh ring out.
I've been there many times before and heard them play beside the pool,
this magic place where no-one goes is where the playful hobbits rule.
And as the seasons come and go and spring or winter greets the day,
if you should visit Sarehole Mill beside the pool the hobbits play.
They've played there now for many years they never age, or so I'm told,
for them eternal youth abounds as I am slowly growing old.

grasping the same feelings that swept through the young Tolkien, feelings which led him to see hobbits peering nervously from dips in the ground, elves scampering mischievously between the bushes and trolls jumping out frighteningly from behind the banks of earth.

Sarehole was a wonderful spot for the childhood of an imaginative boy. Indeed there can be no doubt that Tolkien was deeply affected by the locality and its people, later bringing them into his captivating novels *The Hobbit* and *The Lord of the Rings*. Although born in South Africa, Ronald Tolkien was only three when his dad died and his mom decided to raise her two sons in her native Birmingham. After spending a short time with her parents in Ashfield Road, Kings Heath, the Tolkiens moved to a house at the bottom of Wake Green Road. Behind it lay the magical world of Moseley Bog – overgrown, ancient-looking and entrancing. And across the way was the pond and mill of Sarehole in which lived the 'white ogre', the flour-shrouded miller who often chased off the inquisitive Tolkien lads.

In fact there had probably been millers at Sarehole since the Middle Ages, but certainly they had been present in the area since 1542 when Daniel Benford of Yardley granted John Bedell of Beoley some land and a watercourse on which to erect a mill. Throughout the 1500s it was known as Biddle's Mill after its builder, although it now belonged to the doomed Grevis family of Moseley. By 1727 it was called High Water Mill and was owned by Richard Eaves of Sarehole Farm. He and his descendants did not work the premises, rather they rented them out. Among the tenants was Matthew Boulton who adapted the corn mill for metal rolling before he decided to set up his factory at Soho.

Boulton gave up the tenancy of the mill in 1761 and soon after it was taken down and rebuilt, while the water supply from the Coldbath was supplemented by a headrace. This was cut 800 odd yards up the Cole at Whyrl Hole, close to the Four Arches at the Dingles. For a while, edge tools were ground at the mill as was corn, but by the waking of the nineteenth century the millers had abandoned any industrial use and focused on the making of flour. This task pre-occupied the last millers, the Andrew family. Taking over the tenancy of Sarehole Mill in 1858, they carried on milling until 1919 – although they still lived at the buildings for another 50 years. By this time the mill and the adjoining open space had been left to the City of Birmingham under the will of Mr A.H. Foster.

Following the death of the last of the Andrews it was decided to restore the increasingly dilapidated mill. The job was carried out over five years, carefully led by Gunholt Greiner – a craftsman who was determined to adhere to the skills of the past – and in 1969 Sarehole Mill was ready to be reopened as a branch of the City's Museums and Art Gallery. Today the meadows and pastures which enclosed Sarehole Mill are covered by the houses of Hall Green. But the mill itself remains open and working, the last of over 50 such mills which once stood around Brum. Defiantly and proudly Sarehole Mill bonds us with our rural past.

Gunholt Greiner was the man in charge of the team which renewed Sarehole Mill. German born, he came to Bromsgrove in 1938 as a refugee from the Nazis and spent most of the war working on the land in Scotland. When peace came, he became involved in restoring old buildings and in buying, improving and then selling farms which were run down. With regard to the restoration of places such as Sarehole Mill and a fifteenth century Bromsgrove house which he rebuilt at Avoncroft, Grunner believed that full respect had to be shown to the craftsmen of the past. Thanks to the Birmingham Evening Mail.

The Assembly of the People: The Town Hall

The Town Hall was the pride of Birmingham and it belonged to the people. Sited on that ridge which runs above the northern banks of the River Rea, it drew all eyes to it. Folk were inspired not only by its great size and imposing position but also by its powerful look. As if it were a classical temple, it called out to the times of Ancient Rome and asserted that Brum, too, was now a city state of stature. Birmingham had never boasted such a building.

There were factories which visitors came to see, such as the famed Soho Works of Matthew Boulton and Edward Thomason's 'celebrated establishment' in Church Street where beautiful medals and fine metallic objects were made. There were churches which gained attention, like the superb Saint Philip's designed by Thomas Archer in the Italianate form. There were public buildings like the atmospheric Market Hall. And

A drawing of crowds arriving for a concert at the Town Hall in the mid-1800s. The building on the right was knocked down later to make way for the Council House. Dennis Flynn's grandfather was a stonemason who worked on the Town Hall. He had come from Ireland and reared his children in Summer Lane. As a young boy, Dennis's dad, Sammy, 'would rush home from school at lunch time, gulp down any food going, then run with the old man's dinner all the way up to Snow Hill, along Colmore Row and up the Town Hall steps where old John was waiting for the meal. It was always in a bowl wrapped in a polka dot handkershief and dad was terrified in case it was cold when he delivered it.'

An unusual view of the Town Hall in the late nineteenth century, looking at it from the Easy Row end of Paradise Street and showing clearly Ratcliff Place which ran alongside the building and which featured a cab stand and the statue of James Watt. Nicholas R. Bartleet has happy memories of the annual prize presentations for Saint Philip's Grammar School which were held at the Town Hall in the early 1960s. Nicholas was in the choir and can still remember the rehearsals in the hall with 'our great music master, John Nicholas, playing Bach's Toccata on the magnificent organ and encouraging us to sing out loud so as to be heard up in the galleries. Following this introduction to the Town Hall and its facilities I often popped in during my working days in the city (at Lewis's, another great institution) for part of the lunch-time organ recital often performed by famous organists.' The father of Nicholas, Leslie Bartleet, was born in 1888 and went to King Edward's School Camp Hill. He was present at the Town Hall for the first performance of Elgar's 'Dream of Gerontius'.

then there was the odd grand house which caused some interest, as with that of John Baskerville on Easy Hill. But that was about it. Brum was a place renowned for the style and cunning of its wares not for the design and cleverness of its buildings – that is, until the Town Hall rose up in glory.

Indeed, it was a strange situation. In 1831 Brum had a population of almost 150,000 and was acknowledged as one of the leading towns of the nation – yet it had neither a council nor a major public building. By the end of that decade it had both. The idea of the Town Hall arose because of the Triennial Music Festivals. Held since 1788 to raise money for the General Hospital, then in Summer Lane, many of the concerts took place in the Theatre Royal and Saint Philip's. However, by the 1820s the crowds which were attending the concerts made it obvious that a more suitable venue should be built. Pressurised by the Festival Committee and the ratepayers, the idea of a town hall took hold amongst the Street Commissioners – the body of unelected men which served as Birmingham's only form of local government. Eventually, a location was chosen on Paradise Street, at the top of Hill Street, and Hansom and Welch were taken on as the architects. Work started in 1832 and the Town Hall was opened on September 19, 1834 – although it was not finished properly until 1849 and the later stages of its construction were carried out under the direction of the architect, Charles Edge.

The Town Hall was a stunning building which dominated the skyline of Brum and it was praised as 'a remarkable attempt to apply to modern purposes a style of structure which belonged essentially to the Greek temples'. It had a rusticated basement lined with doorways and upon which were 'a splendid series of Corinthian columns'. Made with brick dug up from the earth of Selly Oak, the whole structure was faced with Anglesey Marble. Sadly two of the workmen employed on the construction were killed when the hook of a pulley block broke. They were buried in St Philip's and in their memory was put up a monument made of the base of a pillar which had been wrought by one of the men.

So soon as it was opened, the Town Hall grabbed the affections of all Brummies because it drew in all kinds of Brummie. It opened its doors not only for renowned classical composers such as Mendelssohn and Elgar but also for leading jazz musicians and pop groups. It was a place where school speech days were held and in which you could listen to politicians and famous writers of the stature of Charles Dickens. The most democratic and egalitarian of buildings in its uses, the Town Hall was the great public meeting place of Birmingham. It will be so once again.

A view of the Town Hall from somewhere near to the General Post Office. The car and boy with the basket carriage are coming down Congreve Street and the Chamberlain Fountain is obvious in the background. Hilda Burnett's most vivid memory of the Town Hall is of the time in 1957 when she attended a Labour party meeting 'and discovered that my hero, Paul Robeson, was the guest of honour. I took my daughter along because he was one of my favourite people from back in the 1930s. He sang all his songs and gave a speech and then led us all in singing The Red Flag. We went backstage later and I got his autograph. He stood upright like a tower of strength – it made my day to meet him. Don't forget, by the way, that Councillor Percy Shurmer used to give great parties for the poor kids in the Town Hall in the 1940s.'

For Roy Whitehouse, the Town Hall meant jazz concerts. As a teenager, jazz wasn't to be heard on the wireless and 'to hear it in the classical splendour of the Town Hall was quite amazing. Not only were there bands from other cities like London, Manchester and Nottingham, but many local lads who'd joined forces. The names that spring to mind include the Gully Low Stompers, Gut Bucket Six and later the Second City Jazz Band. Terry Weir is also a jazz afficionado. His defining moment in life came on June 21, 1952 at 8.00 p.m. when Humphrey Lyttleton's Jazz Band began to play 'Come on and Stomp, Stomp, Stomp' in the Town Hall. At the end of that first number, 'my mate, Gordon Whitworth, and I turned to each other and without saying a word we knew that we had found something very special'.

Birmingham Bertha: The Whirlwind of 1931

They called it Birmingham Bertha, that mighty whirlwind which wreaked destruction as it revolved rapidly across parts of south-east Birmingham on June 14, 1931. It was something so out of the ordinary that only the very old could bring to mind a similar terrifying experience which had occurred back on April 4, 1877. On that day, another column of air had spun rapidly round and round in the vicinity of Coleshill. So furious had it been that it had blown over hayricks, uprooted trees and battered hedges. But Birmingham Bertha did not whirligig across the sparsely-populated countryside. Instead it swept across a densely packed city and so had the capacity for greater pulverisation.

Like the 'twisters' which overwhelmed parts of Bournbrook and Edgbaston in 1999, that inter-war vortex was thrust into being by the elements on a clammy midsummer's day. As the air became heavier and stickier, so did a wind come up. Soon great mountains of clouds darkened out the sun and the forthcoming storm was heralded by the flight of birds. Their escape was followed by a powerful thunderstorm which rent the atmosphere with its booming claps and which scared the skies with its jagged lightning. And again, just like the whirlwinds of 1999, the twister of 1931

The aftermath of the whirlwind on the corner of Palace Road and Green Lane, Bordesley Green. Thanks to Mrs U. Jung. Mrs B.J. Killworth had taken some of her neighbour's little children to Sparkhill Swimming Baths and 'we were walking home when the tornado struck'. It came down Showell Green Lane 'and almost blew us off our feet. Chimney pots, slates, corrugated iron sheets, saucepans and all sorts of rubble flew past. I managed to push the children into the doorway of Wolfson's fur shop on the corner of the road... and I shielded them by hanging on to the large door handle.'

A tree uprooted by the whirlwind of June 1931 in front of houses in Sarehole Road, Hall Green and which backed on to the River Cole. This photograph was taken by Ernest Snelgrove who was on hand with his camera as the tornado swept by. J.F. Cresswell remembers playing cricket in the recreation ground at the junction of Foremans Road and Reddings Lane when 'the clouds came over heavy and it was muggy and there was a copper-coloured sky that I had not seen before in this country. On the recreation ground itself there was a strong wind, but nothing exceptional, when it started to rain we went home. We heard later that a lady had been buried under a wall. Later I went to Sarehole Road, near the College Arms, where the twister had gone down the road in spiral fashion, uprooting some trees. The trees were sizeable, but they had been overturned systematically. Some of my friends' families had minor injuries and shock, but I think only the poor lady died as a result of the storm.'

emerged as if from the ground itself close to a watercourse. In the later twentieth century it was the Bourn Brook, then it was the River Cole.

Starting at the top end of Hall Green close to Springfield, the vortex suddenly took shape in Sarehole Road where it clawed trees up from the ground. With a power which only nature could throw up, the whirlwind swirled over the river, along the allotments at the back of Bromyard Road and into Formans Road, Tyseley. Here it changed direction with all the unpredictability of something over which no man or woman could hope to wrest control. As the frightening force twisted up the hill it blew off the roof of Miss Margaret Seeley's shop. Two doors along, at an outdoor on the corner of Leominster Road, it caused even worse destruction. The side of the building was destroyed so that onlookers could see into the private world of the shopkeeper.

Remorselessly, the whirlwind raced giddily towards Lucas's, blowing off roof tiles, blasting down fences and ferociously chucking upwards loose palings. Across the rec in Reddings Lane it went, literally putting the wind up the lads who were playing football there, and then once again it sought the water of the Cole. Shifting swiftly back downhill, it tore out window frames from the shops opposite the 'Greet Inn' and hurled them over 100 yards away into the yard of the Serck. Sticking tight to the course of the river, the wrecking air stream gyrated alongside what is now the Small Heath Bypass and then rolled onto the Coventry Road as if it were heading towards town. Freed from its watery bond, at Small Heath Park it grabbed out of the earth scores of deep-rooted trees and screamed onwards to damage buildings close to Charles Road.

Carrying with it terror as much as violence, the tornado circled furiously into Muntz Street, where at number 165, the home of the Caswells, it tugged into itself a lilac tree. After grasping it for a few seconds, the whirlwind slung the tree so strongly through the kitchen roof that it split asunder the sink, dresser and mangle. Everywhere, windows were shattered, chimneys were sent hurtling to the ground and soot was shaken around like confetti – whilst the tyres of an Inner Circle 8 bus were strangely stripped from their wheel rims.

Dizzily spinning over one spot for only a few minutes, the vortex closed in on the junction of Green Lane and Palace Road, where real tragedy struck. The woman who ran the corner papershop was killed in her bed. With all the sharp shards of glass whizzing dangerously about, it was a miracle that no-one else died. Whirling and whinnying on its path, the revolving wind carried with it trees, bricks and other flotsam before tossing such wreckage downwards. At last, as it hit Bordesley Green, it lost its vigour and disappeared as mysteriously as it had come. The scenes left behind by the tornado were those which sadly would soon become familiar to Brummies. For the havoc it wrought was similar to that which would be caused by the bombs of the Luftwaffe. Over 50 years separated the whirlwind of Coleshill and that which pounded part of Tyseley and Small Heath. Let's hope that it's at least another 50 odd years before another twister spins itself into being in Brum.

Damage to houses in Formans Road, Sparkhill. Thanks to Ernest Snelgrove. Margaret Jones's aunt lived in what were known as the long gardens in Formans Road. The roof of the family home was blown off by the tornado but fortunately no-one was injured. Margaret recounts that 'my aunt was very lucky, as she had recently had her tonsils out, and she had been told to stay in bed... but for some reason, she had gone downstairs. The chimney pot came through the roof, and through her mother's bed. My dad, and a younger sister were at Sunday School at that time, and my aunt had to go and fetch them, and tell them that they had no home to go back to. They lost everything, including their clothes. My aunt had to borrow clothes to go back to work in. They were given £5 from the Lord Mayor's Fund.

They had to buy black clothes, as they were still in mourning after both my grandfather, and great grandfather had died on the same day just a couple of months before. I believe that temporary accomodation was found for them in Hall Green.' F. V. Moran recalls that all the Catholic children of Sparkhill were looking forward to the annual open air procession in Evelyn Road in honour of the Body and Blood of Christ on Corpus Christi. Then the tornado sprang up and roared past the backs of Esme Road where 'I saw our tall Lombardy Poplar trees bent horizontal. From there it crossed Stratford Road into Hillfield Road where a seven year old schoolgirl saw an elderly man lifted off his feet and carried down the road. It was next in Formans Road where it caused the sidewall of a shop to collapse on a woman trying to shelter there. Finally it went along Formans Road and lifted the roofs off a row of houses and on to Small Heath where it uprooted 200 mature trees in Victoria Park.'